THE BEST THING THAT EVER HAPPENED TO ME

VOLUME 2

JOSEPH C. THEK

ISBN—13: 979-8-9873591-1-2

ISBN—10: 8-98-735911-5

CONTENTS

Preface   v

1. Working and Meeting Dominic   1
2. Funny George and Margot's Place   9
3. Uncle Ray   14
4. Mr. Rufallo   18
5. Money Matters   25
6. Getting into Medical School   30
7. Val Again   33
8. Moving for Medical School   37
9. The Phone Call   42
10. The Shelter   45
11. Two more boys   50
12. Larry Hawley   54
13. Val Again, Again   57
14. More Medical School   59
15. Jimmy Comes Home   65
16. Geisinger   70
17. The Digby Family   76
18. The Helicopter   82
19. Life Outside the ER   85
20. The Second Year at Geisinger   91
21. The Residents' Union   97
22. Bill   102
23. Practical Jokes   107
24. Soccer Coach   115
25. Barry the Big Mouth   118
26. The Conference   123
27. Appendicitis   127
28. Mercy Hospital   130
29. Buying the New House   134
30. Settling In   138
31. Patrick McCarthy   143
32. Ian O'Grady   148
33. Bill Again   155
34. The Highland Avenue House   163
35. The Kids   169

36. Cousin Lena   175
37. Disney World   181
38. Work   185
39. Day Shift   195
40. Evening shift   201
41. The Trip   209
42. Night Shift   217
43. Susie   224
44. The AHA   230
45. Eduardo   239
46. The Office   243
47. The Fire   248
48. Moving On   252
49. Val Again   258
50. The Adventure   264
51. The Second Time   271
52. The Divorce   274

Notes   281

PREFACE

This volume chronicles how I raised a family and became a doctor. I'm still amazed that a kid from New York City with my record could become a doctor. There's only one explanation—I had help. In other words, it's a miracle. It's nothing I did except to say that when I followed HIS rules, then things worked out. I got in trouble when I didn't. Thank GOD for HIS patience with me.

I could have died many times. I should have died. If I had, I would've gone straight to Hell. Now, Heaven is my destination. What could be better than that?

Many of you may wonder, "Did this happen?" The answer, for the most part, is "Yes." In places, I have combined stories and smoothed the rough edges. The dialogue isn't exact, and I didn't mean it to be. The take-home idea is that a conversation like the one described took place, and what was said was something like that.

But there are some stories I left out entirely as being too unbelievable. Truth *is* stranger than fiction.

This volume can be funny in spots, but salvation is no laughing matter. Can the lost laugh? Yes! At the time, I was very lost and didn't know it. But someone's laughter can turn to gloom. Look at the result.

That's not "hate speech." It's telling the truth. I wouldn't bother to tell you if I wasn't concerned about your final eternal home. But when I do, I should do it with love[1].

We have been visited by an extra-terrestrial being named JESUS, the Christ. It took me years and a broken life to get humbly down on my knees until all the pieces fit together. To see how all that happened to this sinner—read on.

1

WORKING AND MEETING DOMINIC

I had a son. Josh had long fingernails and a full head of black hair, which was more than I could say for my sparse blond hair. Everything had changed. Before, I could be carefree, only answering for Edie and myself. Now, I had additional responsibilities. Another life dependent on me did that. I should have felt the Hand of GOD in my life, but stubbornly, I didn't.

I lacked money, and the future was questionable.

What potential do I have? Being a young Saul Alinsky can't support a family. I have to change.

My alternatives were medicine and law. Both provided a career while I raised a family.

So what if I have no experience in either? Get in law or medical school some way. After all, I spent three years with the farm workers. Anything is possible!

While reading Somerset Maugham's *Of Human Bondage*, I was impressed.

Now Philip is a real hero. He realizes that his painting will never support him, so he becomes a doctor. Not a bad idea. That way, I can make a living and help others.

When I reflect upon it now, I'm sure GOD was looking over my shoulder the whole time. I wasn't reading the Bible then, so GOD influenced me through Somerset Maugham.

But what about my arrests? Maybe they won't ask.

They never did.

I tried to reason things out.

Don't have a lot of time. Be twenty-five when I start. But have a ton of science credits from NCE. Can use them if I go pre-med. Medicine it is!

WATERGATE WAS IN THE NEWS. Nixon was getting his comeuppance. We stayed glued to the TV and the Senate hearings. I should not have been. GOD has everything in HIS mighty hands, and there is no need to worry. That understanding came to me many years later. To show you how caught up with this world I was, I celebrated on the night Nixon resigned. Rather than see the futility of it all, I chose a side. I didn't see or understand that when one loses, we all lose. Life was a giant "Who" and "What" game.

Now, I think that life is a long lesson. The test follows on Judgment Day. It's great to know the results ahead of time!

We are all called to repentance. It's throughout the Bible. In both the Old Testament[1] and the New Testament[2]. The message today is the same as it was then. Will we ever listen?

EDIE AND I quit the farm workers, and we moved in with my parents. She was twenty, and I was all of twenty-three.

They should have courses to teach you how to be a good parent.

I enrolled on the final day of admission at Paterson State College. Another day and I would've missed the whole semester. Coincidence? I think not.

Up until then, Paterson State was a teachers' college. It had a pre-med program and was cheap. It cost three hundred and seventy-five dollars for my third year because the scholarship paid half the tuition.

Living with my parents lasted a couple of months. We lived upstairs in my old bedroom. However, we ate our meals downstairs with them.

Jap, the father of a union supporter, Wayne Rutley, was a chef at a local restaurant that catered weddings and big parties.

Wayne gave him our number.

"Hello?" my mother answered the phone one afternoon.

After a few moments, she put her hand across the receiver and yelled, "Joseph! It's for you!"

"No need to yell. I'm right here," I replied from my seat at the dining room table in the next room where I'd been reading, wondering what direction my life would go in now.

"Hello?" I answered. *Who could this be?*

"This is Jap Rutley," came the reply.

Jap? Is he Asian?

"Wayne's father."

The mud started to get clearer.

"Understand you may be looking for work. Want a job?" he asked.

"Why, yes, I do." I was too stupid to see the Hand of Providence working. The salary wasn't much, but it allowed us our own place.

Mostly, I cut tomatoes, stuffed capons, scooped ice cream, loaded the dishwasher, or scrubbed pots and pans.

Jap and I were the only kitchen staff who spoke English. The waiters were Iranian, and the kitchen helpers were from China and Poland. The Chinese went down to the Passaic River and stared into the water, then, with a quick motion, put a hand in the moving water to catch a fish.

The Chinese lived above the kitchen, and the boss paid them off the books. Leo, the owner-boss, was a little bald man who hardly ever smiled. He always fought with the Chinese about overtime. He refused to pay it and made out like the thief he was.

Orientals, Iranians, Poles, Americans – we are all people. We need GOD to point that out to us.

"You pay!" one of the Chinamen yelled at Leo one pay-day.

Leo became angry, pulled a can down from a shelf, and maced him in the kitchen!

"I get you!" the Chinaman exclaimed and went after him with a kitchen knife.

Jap intervened. Throwing up his hands to halt the Chinaman, he shielded Leo. Jap courageously barked, "Whoa! Put that down before someone gets hurt!"

The boss didn't know how close he was to dying.

I joined the Chinese in hating Leo. It was hard not to. Any possible way, I would get revenge. I wasn't aware of what it was doing to me.

An opportunity arose when I stuffed a carton of milk for Josh under my shirt. Somehow, I thought that was a blow to his body.

Show him!

Leo was waiting for me in the parking lot.

"What have you got there?" he asked, nodding toward my bulging shirt.

I sheepishly revealed the carton of milk.

"Well, well," he said. "What were you gonna do with that?"

Recovering, I said, "It's late. The stores are closed. Wanted to *borrow* some for my son."

"Sure, you were," he squinted. "Have to take it out of your pay."

"Was gonna suggest that."

Leo snorted. "And why did you put it under your shirt?"

"It's scorching out. Wanted to keep my body cool."

"That's a good one," Leo laughed uncharacteristically. "You're lucky I like you, Thek."

Him liking me is a curse. What am I doing wrong?

He moved out of my way.

On the way home, I remembered something Dad had claimed. "If you steal a little, you're a worker. If you steal a lot, you're an owner."

I quit. Working in the steaming kitchen was grueling. It made the summer heat seem cool.

I needed money, so I started caddying again. The greens' crew hired me to dig ditches. There is always a need for a strong back and a healthy constitution. Eventually, I became the water boy.

Being a caddy and a greens keeper had its advantages. If a golfer angered me while I was caddying some afternoon, the next day, I'd put the hole near the crest of a hill of a bi-level green in the early morning while I cut the green. When I caddied afterward, I chuckled silently as the golfer missed the hole and the ball rolled down the hill.

"Look where the *#*# greens keeper put the hole!" cursed the golfer. "If I get my hands of him, I'll wring his neck! Now I'm gonna four-putt! This isn't miniature golf!"

Don't mess with me., I'd think and smile. However, who was I messing with?

I didn't act like a Christian then. Old habits like "an eye for an eye"[3] are hard to overcome.

Revenge is sweet.

But, who does it really affect?

I BECAME the water boy in the late afternoon during the hot summer. I drove a sprinkler cart down the middle of the fairway. If a golfer had stiffed me the day before while caddying, I watered the hole ahead of him. If the golfer wanted a decent score, he had to play in the water. If he really riled me, I preceded him around the whole course. I'd sprinkle one hole at a time, so he spent his entire day playing in the water. I was not one to get angry. In retrospect, it wasn't a Christian thing to do. We are all sinners, saved by grace.

I particularly remember one night. It happened to be my twenty-fourth birthday and I was in a hurry to get home where an ice cream cake awaited me. It was about eight in the evening and I had to remove the sprinklers from the ninth hole before dark. It was on a slight upgrade, so I climbed out and let the cart roll to me to save time. The wheels turned. The cart started to roll right for the sprinkler head! Without thinking, I put my leg between the sprinkler head and the cart. I was pinned between the two. There I was at dusk, in the middle of the fairway, with the water still running soaking me.

At first, I laughed. Then I realized no one would find me until morning. It was no longer a laughing matter.

"Help!" I yelled repeatedly.

About nine o'clock (Time must be Irish), someone at a party in the clubhouse heard me screaming. The sprinkler trapped me against the cart for about an hour. It could have been much worse. After I was released, I turned off the sprinklers and went to my nearby, parent's house.

It was worse there. Dad had trimmed the bushes in front of the house earlier in the day and related this story.

"'Say, do you wanna borrow my electric hedge-cutter?' Mr. Ross (a neighbor) asked when he saw me struggling.

"'Sure.' I looked at it and wondered how it worked.

"When I finally figured out how to turn it on, I started to cut. Then, suddenly, the power went out."

"What happened?" I muttered."

"I looked. I hadn't cut just the bushes, but the cord too! Mr. Ross was not too pleased when I returned it."

"That's not all," Mom interjected after Dad had finished telling his story. "I backed into the car across the street."

"How'd you do that?" I asked trying not to laugh at Dad's story.

"Mrs. Lookout (their neighbor across the street) parked her car directly behind our driveway for some reason. It was not in her driveway. I didn't see it and plowed right into it when I backed out of our driveway."

"Were you hurt?"

She shook her head. "Nobody was."

Now you know from whom I get my expertise!

Edie and I finally sat at the dining room table with them for our ice cream cake.

Edie and I knew a Margot Hummer in Weehawken. She supported the farm workers, ran a Peace Center, and a boarding house. We moved into it. From there, I could commute to school.

When I started at Paterson State (Now it was called William Paterson College. I guess the college didn't want to be associated with the city of Paterson.), the instructors didn't know what to make of me. I was an unknown being in pre-med, and a transfer from NCE three and a half years earlier.

I was unconventional.

Once, a bee flew into the organic chemistry lab. The other students yelled, "Kill it! Kill it!"

"Wait!" I interrupted.

I placed a Styrofoam cup over the bee. Then, I put a piece of cardboard over the mouth of the cup. Now that I had the insect captured, I went to the window, set the cup outside, and let it go.

Afterwards, I had a new lab partner, called Joe Robistelli. Through Joe, I met Dominic Ruffalo. He was taking Organic Chemistry, too, but more importantly, lived in West New York near Weehawken. We could drive together.

On the first day, Dominic and I were supposed to have an Organic quiz. He picked me up in his sister's Volkswagen beetle. It snowed. Dominic took the back roads. He lost control and the car slid down a hill.

"Are you hurt?" he asked after we hit a parked car and stopped.

"Nope."

Dominic and I missed the Organic quiz.

Maybe I should commute with someone else. But the accident wasn't his fault. It could've happened to anybody.

The decision to stay led to a long relationship with him. He was in pre-med, too. Dominic, born in Genoa, emigrated to the U.S. when he was nine, learned Spanish before English, and became my good friend.

Dominic was a year behind me in college. His girlfriend, Aracely Sanchez, was born in Cuba. Every date was chaperoned, mostly by her older sister, even after they were engaged. Theirs was a whole different world.

He was a big guy–weighing over 200 pounds and nearly as tall as me. Dominic wanted me to major in biology. He joined its club, and, because of his size, was even on the Biology basketball team. One time, he asked me "Why don't you come watch our game?"

So, I did.

It was a close game. Back and forth went the score. It was tied with a couple seconds to play. However, Dominic had yet to be in the game. The first-string forward fouled out. Dominic replaced him. This was his chance to be a hero after languishing on the bench! When the opposition threw the ball in, he stole it, took one step and heaved before he went out of bounds.

Swish!

What a shot! Nothing but net!

The buzzer sounded. The one problem being it was the wrong basket! Dominic had scored two points for the other team and they won.

2

FUNNY GEORGE AND MARGOT'S PLACE

Through Dominic, I met "Funny" George Castano. His family was unusual. George's uncle was serving time in prison as a hit man for the Mafia. Even in prison, the Castano family admired him.

George wanted to get out of the Air Force. First, he pretended to be a plane. When he finally stopped swinging his arms like propellers, he wouldn't set foot on an airplane. No one could coax him on one. In the Air Force, that's not a good thing. You can't have your pilots refusing to go near a plane.

He got thrown out of the Air Force for being crazy.

Pretty good act if he's faking it.

When George went to Europe, he bought a motorcycle and toured the countryside.

"Where is Canada?" a traveler asked him.

"I'm not sure," George replied, even though it is only one state away from Rutherford, New Jersey, where he lived. That ignorance inspired him to want to be pre-med. It also earned him the nickname "Funny." George was – well – weird.

I accompanied George, Tommy Thek, Michael Ventra, and Dave

Triolo to New Hampshire to climb Mt. Washington. Johnny was under the weather. At least, that's what he said.

Oh great! Tommy and Dave again! What will it be this time?

We stopped at a lean-to near the timberline. We returned to Mount Washington in early November.

THIS IS a second chance for me.

A second chance? Only a fool would try it again. However, it was a lot warmer than the first time. We now climbed the other side, away from Canada's high winds.

Get you this time.

Get who? A mountain could care less if it could care.

George put on his backpack at the lean-to near the base of Tuckerman's Ravine[1].

"What are you doing?" I asked casually.

"I'm going up," he replied, pointing at the immense wall of nearly vertical rock.

"Up there? It's steep and dangerous."

"Want to practice hiking." He ascended like it was just a trip around the block.

When George returned, we settled down in our sleeping bags. Dave owned an Eddie Bauer sleeping bag, which could withstand the elements.

"I don't need an Eddie Bauer," Tommy began, "it's not that cold."

Here we go!

"And it isn't raining," Tommy continued. "Or, snowing,"

"All right, all right! We'll see who needs it when it is," Dave retorted.

"This is the Northeast, not the Rockies," Tommy smirked. "Besides, we're in a lean-to."

"Are you forgetting our last trip?" I asked.

"That was then. This is now," my cousin answered like that somehow made sense.

Tommy continued to jibe at him. I don't think Dave slept that night because of it, Eddie Bauer or not.

In the morning, we climbed the mountain. Tuckerman's Ravine wasn't exactly The Dike, but it was steep. However, it had a trail. We couldn't get in trouble if we stayed on it. After a few hours of hiking, we finally reached the summit.

They had an old rock cabin at the top. Tommy and I entered. On a dais was an open book for people who had done the climb. We wrote in our names. Beside it was a space for the place of origin. Without second thoughts, we both scribbled in "Aachen, Germany.[2]"

Finally, beat it!

We exited and tried to keep on our feet because it was windy.

We climbed down to the camp. I was satisfied.

No mountain can beat a Thek!

Who was I kidding? Mountains don't think. Even if they could, they would wonder why fools climb them.

"Let's go into town," I remarked.

"And break camp?" George asked.

"Yeah. We could get a motel room for the night," I continued, undaunted.

"Really communing with Mother Nature," Dave scoffed. "No thanks. I'm tired. I'd rather stay right here."

"Besides, you have nothing to be afraid of with your Eddie Bauer," Tommy ridiculed.

"Laugh if you want," Dave replied. "At least I'm prepared."

"And I'm not?" Tommy shouted.

Better defuse this situation. Things could get ugly.

I rose and started to walk.

Turning toward me, Dave asked, "Where are *you* going?"

"Into Conway, you can stay here if you want."

George and Dave camped again under the stars. A bit romantic. They made me want to stick a finger down my throat.

Tommy, Michael, and I had enough of roughing it. We hiked to the bottom and stayed in a motel in Conway. The three of us visited several fast-food restaurants because we couldn't decide what to eat, so Tommy, Michael, and I chose everything. We were non-discriminating.

George and I became good friends despite the camping trip.

I MAJORED in chemistry with a minor in biology. Dominic eventually switched to it, also. I received all A's in the first semester. I transferred from NCE with a cumulative average of 3.18. Now, it was over 3.3.

I began to study for the MCAT[3]s to be accepted into medical school. While in college, Edie made outlines of the books I read. I even took a course to improve my grades.

The other students were nervous on the morning of the test, but I wasn't. I had a son and couldn't afford to be. I moved away from them. Their anxiety could be contagious. I know now that GOD was behind me.

The MCATs were like the SATs, except there were four parts; English, History, Science, and Math.

The scores for each four were based on a perfect eight hundred. Anything above five hundred was good. When my scores came back, my low was five hundred sixty for Science (I hadn't taken all of the courses yet), and my high was seven hundred ten in Math.

Suddenly, I was a celebrity, and everyone wanted to know me, even teachers who were aloof before. They *wanted* me in medical school. I would take a flagging pre-med program that had never before placed anyone in medical school and deliver it myself. But it wasn't me at all. GOD had me in the palm of HIS hand all along. I was just too stupid and proud to realize it.

I applied, concentrating on schools in or near New Jersey since the reciprocity with other states was poor.

WE WERE STILL LIVING at Margot's. One of her tenants, Hannah Manson, lived on the third floor and had several annoying habits, like leaving her alarm clock set. It went off in the evening and not in the morning. Hannah couldn't seem to understand the difference between a.m. and p.m. For weeks, I had to climb the stairs to the third floor, enter her room, and turn the alarm off. After several trips, I was tired of hearing it.

One evening, precisely at six, I was in the kitchen on the first floor when her radio started blasting away. Hannah wasn't home yet from work to shut it off. So, I climbed the stairs to the third floor.

I'll get her!

I threw the alarm clock out of the window. It was a factual case of seeing time fly.

The following week, I was eating my lunch at work one afternoon when I noticed something amiss in the Oreos that Edie, as usual, had packed.

What's this?

The creamy white centers were missing!

What happened?

Hannah had eaten them and then put the brown tops and bottoms back together! When she left, there was no love lost. Hannah later became a lawyer.

The Kobels (Lee, Tamara, and son, Daniel) replaced her. Before, they had rented the farm where Edie and I were married.

The Kobels were good people. When Lee came down with Job's syndrome (staph boils all over his body), Tamara never complained. She kept on being Tamara and raised their son.

3

UNCLE RAY

Margot drove an old Volkswagen beetle with bumper stickers covering it.

"They're keeping your car together," I said.

One afternoon, Margot stopped to pick up a hitchhiker in New Jersey on the way to her farmhouse in upstate New York. He was unusual, in his fifties, slightly older than she. The hitchhiker wore checkered pants that didn't match his checked shirt. He would tell jokes at Eddy's Farm, not far from where she was going.

The conversation turned to the bumper stickers on her car. "I have a nephew who boycotts lettuce," the hitchhiker commented.

"You do? What's his name?"

"Joe Thek."

Margot was flabbergasted. Without knowing it, she had picked up my Uncle Ray - younger brother of Dad's!

Uncle Ray was an athlete. He went to grammar school with the future governor of New York. Uncle Ray received a basketball scholarship to Princeton, where he met the future governor of New Jersey. Uncle Ray was in both the New York City police *and* fire departments.

Dad told me this story about Uncle Ray. "During WW II, he was drafted into the army and was in the Battle of the Bulge. His squad was cut off from the other Americans. Bullets started to fly, so they jumped into a foxhole. A potato masher, a grenade, landed in it. Ray dove on top of his commander in an attempt to save the sergeant's life. However, the potato masher rolled under the officer. It exploded, killing the sergeant, but Ray was not scratched. In effect, he saved himself at the expense of another.

"Ray was never the same. He drank. I bailed him out when we received phone calls from local jails."

Uncle Ray bragged to the police officers after being booked one night. "I went to school with two governors and was in the New York Police and the New York Fire Department."

The police officers stuffed his head into a toilet and flushed it because they didn't believe him. Every word was accurate. Well, almost, he could exaggerate a wee mite. Dad hated the police because of it.

"They were mean to him," he said, matter-of-factly. "They didn't have to be. Your uncle never hurt anybody."

He brought us copper wiring that he had gotten in New York City and dumped it in a pile in our basement beside a growing mound of his other junk. "Someday, it will sell," he assured us. Nothing he brought us ever did.

Once, on Long Island, when I was about eight, my father drove with Uncle John, his oldest brother, and Uncle Ray, his youngest, in the car. We were in the back going to see Uncle Pete, Aunt Henrietta, and Tommy. *En route*, Uncle John had a coughing spell because he suffered from emphysema.

Dad stopped alongside the highway.

"Better get out and put your arms of the car," Dad suggested.

Uncle Ray had to slide out of the car first to let Uncle John move past him. While he waited with Uncle John's arms propped on the car's roof, Uncle Ray took his own wallet out to see how much money he had.

A passing cop stopped.

"Freeze!" he shouted while he pulled his gun from his holster and pointed it at Uncle Ray.

Uncle Ray was startled and dropped the wallet on the ground.

"What the—"

"Hands up!" the nervous cop yelled.

Uncle Ray staring at a gun wasn't going to argue. He put his hands in the air and spread-eagled.

"You're not gonna rob this man!" the cop yelled.

"Rob him? I was doing no such thing! He's my brother!"

I envisioned bailing him out of some dark and dingy Long Island jail.

Finally, Uncle John stopped coughing long enough to verify the truth of Uncle Ray's statement.

As I said, Uncle Ray was an athlete. One time, we played golf, and Uncle Ray pulled out his driver on the fifth tee. There were trees to the right of it. When he hit, the ball struck one of the trunks squarely and bounced back toward him. Uncle Ray caught it in his bare hand and teed up the ball again. He teed up and hit the ball again in one motion like he expected it to happen. This time, it soared down the middle of the fairway. How could you penalize someone after that?

Uncle Ray didn't have any visible means of support - a genuine vagrant. Edie was sure Uncle Ray worked for the CIA. Pretty good cover if he did.

One of his friends died, naming him executor of the will. How could someone expect him to settle anything? It included a pop-up tent on top of a small trailer. It resided beside our garage. Uncle Ray certainly didn't have any place to store it.

Then, he died in a car crash near Suffern, New York. Dad was devastated; it was the second time I had seen him cry. Dad became the executor of Uncle Ray's will. He had been driving drunk—they don't mix. However, no one else was injured.

At the funeral, a woman named Betty appeared. We discovered that Uncle Ray had lived with her for a long time. He was driving her car the night of the accident. Dad conferred with my Uncle Pete.

After speaking with Uncle Pete, Dad said to Betty, "Here, we want the inheritance to be yours."

"How much of it?"

"It's not much. A few grand. You can have it all."

"I don't know what to say."

"Then don't say anything. Just take the money."

Uncle Ray would have liked that.

In effect, Betty was Uncle Ray's widow. Dad just did what was right for her. I never forgot it. [1]

4

MR. RUFALLO

I wanted to get our own place. Margot's was excellent, but there was no telling when another Hannah could move in.

When Dominic's tenants moved out of the first story, Gilda, his older sister, moved from the first-floor apartment in his house to the second floor with her children. That left the first-floor apartment (partly below ground) empty, and we wanted to move into it. I was in my senior year at William Paterson, awaiting a response to my application to medical school. They also had a big driveway where we could park our car alongside Dominic's father's truck and behind his sister's Volkswagen. That was the only driveway on the block.

I met Dominic's maternal grandfather, Mr. Macaluso. As an older man, he was now a crossing guard for the local school children. However, as a young man during World War II, Mr. Macaluso piloted his own merchant boat. He was torpedoed and sunk three times in the Mediterranean, twice by the English and once by the Germans. Early in the war, Italy had been an ally of Nazi Germany. However, after the Italian dictator, Mussolini was executed, they became enemies. I don't know how the grandfather survived with everybody shooting at him. I guess Mr. Macaluso could swim.

Afterward, his daughter married Mr. Ruffalo, had two children and moved to America. Mr. Macaluso and his wife followed later.

Dominic's father was actually born in Carteret, New Jersey. How he came to be in Italy to meet Mrs. Ruffalo is a story.

Mr. Ruffalo, when he was young, was in a card game one night. This is the way he told the story in his broken English.

"Two-a guys got into fight. 'You cheat!' one yelled. 'Did-a not!' the other yelled back. One-a guy takes out gun. He puts in other guy's chest. Gun goes off. Bam! Other guy falls to ground. Blood everywhere. He dead. I scared. Run. Cops chase me. Arrest me. They send me to jail in Italy."

"But I thought you were born here," I said.

"No matter. Send me anyway."

Mr. Ruffalo went to prison in Italy. When he got out, he was drafted by the Italian Army just before they invaded Yugoslavia during early WW II. Once, the Yugoslavs ambushed his platoon. Thirteen of them hid under a giant boulder. They fired a mortar at them, killing twelve instantly. Only Mr. Ruffalo survived, and he wondered why they spared him.

One day, he was fighting on the side of Germany. The next day, after Mussolini was executed, Mr. Ruffalo was their enemy. He greeted the German soldiers coming to arrest him! He sat out most of the war in a German POW camp.

After the war, he met Mrs. Ruffalo in Italy, and they married in Genoa, where they had two children (Gilda and Dominic).

Mr. Ruffalo liked Mussolini. I couldn't say derogatory things about the dictator in his presence, even though the man had died thirty years before.

Years later, Dominic told me the story of hunting with his father and his fifteen-year-old nephew, big-boy Angelo, as we traveled together to college. "Once we went hunting deer. My father, being small, insisted we cover him with leaves and leave him in a ditch. We did. He says he saw something brown, so he shot it, thinking it was a deer. But it wasn't a deer. It was a cow!

"We had to tell the farmer what had happened. It maybe funny now, but it certainly wasn't then. The farmer was real, mad. He made Dad pay for it.

"Getting the cow home was a real problem. It was too big for the small bay in the back of the truck. No matter what we did, it couldn't fit. We were just about to give up.

"Then Angelo says, 'Why not put the cow on the hood?'

"That's what we did. Between the three of us, we got the cow on the hood.

"When we piled in the truck, my father said, 'Can't see,' and looked at me.

"'Oh no, not me! I've never driven a stick before!'

"'You learn,' Dad said.

"Well, I took the keys. Between stripping the gears and straining to look over the cow, I was what you call a real 'basket case.'

"On the way home, the head kept sticking out over the side. I dreamed about those cow eyes that night! People we passed gave us some strange looks. After all, how many people do you see with a cow on their hood?

"Then, we tried to convince my mother that the cow was really a deer.

"'Where's antlers?' she asked. "Looks like cow."

She didn't buy it for a second. Then the story came out.

"We ate hamburgers and steaks for months."

I had to laugh.

Then, we moved into the small first-story apartment. There were three rooms besides the kitchen and bathroom. We put a foam rubber mattress on the floor in one of them. If we shut the door, it wouldn't fit.

Josh stayed in another, which gave us a living room in the third. They were cozy. At least, that's how Edie and I defined them.

But there was no place to study. Finally, I improvised. The boiler room was the quietest place in the house once you got past the noise of the boiler. It was almost serene. So, I studied there. It was just off our apartment. If Edie needed me, I was nearby.

Dominic drove me a couple of times a week to college when we had the same classes. We had a cold winter that year. I used to take the car's battery in at night to ensure it would crank in the morning.

Next to the apartment was a huge garage at the end of their driveway. It was like a small warehouse. I could see it from my above-ground window in our bedroom. Mr. Ruffalo rented it out. We never saw the people who rented it, but someone was using it because new merchandise appeared in it almost daily. One night, I had trouble sleeping, which was very unusual. As I lay there trying to switch my mind off, lights appeared in his driveway. Looking at the clock, it was 3 a.m.!

Who could this be?

I peeked out of the drawn blinds. Edie, awakened by my movement, poked me on the shoulder.

"What's up?" she asked sleepily.

"Shh! Somebody's here," I whispered.

Two men with their collars turned up, opened the garage, and dropped something off. It looked like a TV or stereo. Then they left.

"Who were they?" Edie asked.

"Must be the guys who rented the garage."

"At this hour of the morning?"

I shrugged my shoulders and went back to sleep.

A couple of weeks later, Mr. Ruffalo got suspicious mail.

"What's a this?" he said when I went for my mail in their third-story apartment. He threw the other envelopes on the kitchen table. Dominic opened it and said something to his father in Italian. The two had a brief conversation. Then Mr. Ruffalo left the kitchen holding his head. I wondered what was going on.

Pulling Dominic aside, I asked, "What's in the mail?"

"It's about the tenants," he whispered. "They are Mafioso. All the goods in the garage are stolen. He has to go to court."

"But he can't speak English well. How will he defend himself?

Dominic pointed to his chest. "Me. I'll be his interpreter."

Mr. Ruffalo was very nervous. "I no wanna go back to Italy!" he kept moaning from the adjacent room.

Mr. Ruffalo's salt and pepper hair seemed to have turned all white while he waited. So did his mustache. Finally, the day arrived, and the father and son dressed up in suits and went to court.

Mr. Ruffalo's nervousness was contagious. I looked out the window every five minutes. Edie realized that there was nothing to do and waited patiently.

After several hours Dominic and his father pulled the car into their driveway. One look at Mr. Ruffalo's face told me the verdict. He couldn't stop grinning.

I went from the apartment to greet them in the driveway.

When Mr. Ruffalo saw me, he shouted, "No guilty! And my son-a did it all!"

With that, he took Dominic in his arms and kissed him on both cheeks. Dominic turned red. He was embarrassed because the neighbors could see the whole thing.

"What did you do?" I asked.

"Tell you inside. Not here."

We entered the house, my curiosity exploding within me. We went upstairs to their third-story apartment. Dominic took me to the living room and said, "Sit down."

Mr. Ruffalo said something to his wife in Italian. She came into the room and kissed Dominic on the cheeks. I couldn't contain it any longer, "What happened?"

"It was no big deal," Dominic replied as his parents left the room. "I interpreted a few questions for my father. Then, I noticed that the judge was a Hispanic and thought he was, *Probably from Cuba, like my girlfriend*. So, I asked him how he was in Spanish.

"You would've thought I gave him a million bucks. His whole face changed. It seemed like he couldn't wait to throw the case out of court.

"And now, my father gives me all the credit. He thinks I saved him from an Italian jail."

Dominic was too modest. Perhaps he had.

As I said, the boiler room was adjacent to the apartment. One night, Dominic and I brought a cat home from the Comparative Anatomy lab to dissect and work on it. We looked like two mad scientists. The formaldehyde smell filled the air.

Mr. Ruffalo burst in very agitated. He yelled something in Italian.

Dominic yelled back also in Italian.

Mr. Ruffalo then screamed at his son.

I looked at Dominic quizzically. Then the son and father talked in the foreign tongue for some minutes. Finally, Mr. Ruffalo left.

"What was that all about?" I asked as we went back to work.

"Dad thought we killed the neighbor's cat and were dissecting it in his boiler room!"

We laughed, but that man was dangerous.

Then there was the ice incident. The Ruffalos ran out of ice, so Mr. Ruffalo went to the local gas station to get some. He couldn't remember the English word "ice," so he said the Italian word "*ici*." The attendant couldn't understand him. So, Mr. Ruffalo decided to act it out. He shivered and kept saying, "*Ici! Ici!*"

The gas station attendant thought he was saying, "Itchy! Itchy!" and shivering because of bugs.

"Get out, now!" he screamed.

Mr. Ruffalo was confused. All he wanted was a bag of ice. So, again he said, "*Ici, ici!*" and exaggerated his shivering down to the ground.

"That does it! If you don't leave, I'm calling the cops!" the attendant yelled.

Mr. Ruffalo heard "cops," became scared, and left.

He never did get the ice.

I MAINLY TOOK chemistry and biology courses in my senior year with Dominic. Once, in the Inorganic Chemistry lab, Dominic and I mixed the ingredients for the cleaning solutions, *aqua regia*[1], backward.

Dr. Ryerson, our Inorganic Chemistry professor, erupted into the room. "Get out, now!"

Once outside, we asked, "Why?"

"Because you liberated chlorine gas, you *#*# jerks! They had to evacuate the whole building! I may lose my job because of you two!"

Dominic leaned over and whispered to me, "Don't let my father know."

"I won't," I whispered in return.

Mr. Ruffalo would have been embarrassed if he had found out. But,

Dr. Ryerson didn't get fired, and Mr. Ruffalo never discovered our little secret. The bond between Dominic and me was stronger because of it.

MR. RUFFALO PASSED on many years later of painful prostate cancer. He was a good man and very proud of his children. He was an example to me of how a father is supposed to be.

5

MONEY MATTERS

I n the winter of 1974-75, we needed some money.
Now how will I get enough for my family? What skills do I have? Maybe I'll use my brains? But how?

Danny Fairbanks was a student who used a wheelchair. No one expected him to live very long. But he was taking Organic Chemistry —a challenging course. Professor Satchel, our Organic Chemistry professor, was against his even trying.

"He's taking a space of a student who can go the distance. Danny never will," Dr. Satchel said. "I know what we can do. Thek?"

"Yes, Sir."

"Are you doing anything tonight?"

"Why n-no," I stammered, becoming suspicious.

"Good. I want you to go to Danny Fairbanks' house and give him remedial classes, so he doesn't have to come to my class."

"Can I do that?"

"Sure can, as long as I okay it."

That evening, I went to his house. His mother met me at the door.

"Thanks for coming over! Danny is so excited," she said.

He was an absolute joy to teach. Like a sponge, Danny wanted to absorb everything he could. I understood him plainly. It was unfortunate that he was using a wheelchair. Or was it? Danny was a good role model for me. But I didn't know it yet.

I instructed Danny with molecule models that I had.

"Do you know where you're going when you die?" he asked abruptly during the lesson.

"In the ground," came my rapid reply. I continued angrily, and before censoring my speech, "I'm supposed to ask the questions. Who's the teacher here?"

Danny just shook his head and smiled.

I knew what he meant. *Another Jesus freak.*

When it came time to pay, I couldn't ask him for money. The lesson was for free. That's how my tutoring career began.

Eventually, Danny passed on, but he had planted the seed. It would take many years to bloom.

The other student was a high-school sophomore, Julia Brandt. She was a doctor's daughter. I had done such an excellent job with Danny that somehow the word got around that I was available through the college.

"Whatcha gonna teach me tonight?" she said while blowing a piece of bubble gum. In the months I taught her, Julia always dressed in the latest fad – hot pants or bell bottoms if it was cold. And vests—she had one for every occasion.

I couldn't have cared less, and was all business. Then Doctor Brandt, her father, entered the room unseen during a geometry lesson the first night. Because I didn't notice him, I continued.

"A right triangle is one—" I stopped short in the middle of the sentence on becoming aware of his presence.

He was a big man, taller than me and bulky–not fat, but muscular. I was intimidated.

"Go on, go on," he said, waving his hand. "Pretend I'm not here."

"Now, Daddy, how do we do that?" Julia asked.

"Just making sure I'm getting my money's worth, Sweetheart. By the way, how much is it?"

"I don't think we should discuss business in front of your daughter," I answered.

"Perhaps you're right," he replied. "My apologies." He started to leave.

"No, no," I said. "Please stay. We were just finishing."

"I can take a hint," Julia said and left the room.

When his daughter had gone, Doctor Brandt took out his wallet and asked, "How much?"

I saw many bills in his wallet. Pure and straightforward greed motivated me. The usual fee was $15/hour, but I answered, "$30/hour."

"That's a little steep, isn't it?"

"You get what you pay for."

"Isn't that the truth," he laughed, gave me three twenties, and then left the room. He didn't know it, but he was paying for Danny, too.

I grew to like Julia, but not her teenage moods. One week she wanted to be a talk-show host. The following week she was into neuro-surgery.

"You know that takes years of hard work," I'd say.

"Not for me then. Maybe I could be a singer."

"I didn't know you could sing."

"Didn't know that was required. I mean, look at Mick Jagger. Or Bob Dylan."

"Maybe you're right," I laughed. "When you're famous, maybe you can do one of my songs."

"Your songs? You know music?"

"No. I just write the words."

"Let me hear one."

So, the next time I brought my guitar and played one song called *Simple Soldier*.

I AM A SIMPLE SOLDIER,
    Still, quiet, and forlorn,
    And I am growing older
    Tired, beaten, and worn.
    I will not be much bolder
    I will remain a pawn,

I am a simple soldier
I'm waiting for the dawn,
Waiting for the dawn.

I AM A SIMPLE SOLDIER,
Holding so fast my gun,
My body growing colder
Ragged, wetter, and numb.
The dream I had to shoulder
Now it has come undone,
I am a simple soldier
I'm waiting for the sun,
Waiting for the sun.

I AM A SIMPLE SOLDIER,
I'm trying to keep warm,
An ember left to smolder
Alone here in this storm.
A flag, they will unfold her
Taps played from a horn,
I am a simple soldier
I'm waiting to be born,
Waiting to be born.

IT WAS hard to be a tutor and friend. At least, it is for me. I always got too involved emotionally. So, I stopped tutoring.

I knew that we needed another source of income, so I figured to give unemployment a shot. I hoped to collect partial benefits because greens keeping was a spring and summer job. I would be back at it in a couple of months.

I waited to apply in line for hours. There was a glass partition on a countertop with several breaks where people gave their information. People had their claims settled one by one, and the line inched forward. It was slow, but there was an ending in sight. Finally, it was my turn. The lady at the desk never made eye contact with me.

"Name and social security," she said brusquely without looking up from the papers on her desk. With her hair tied up in a bun and a big scar on her left cheek uncovered, the clerk looked like someone from a Boris Karloff movie. Add to that; she had the personality of cardboard.

No wonder she keeps her head down.

"I'm a full-time student," I tried to explain to her. "But I'll be rehired in the spring. Can I get partial unemployment benefits?"

The lady rose to her long filing cabinets and thumbed through folders. It took some time to get any information because this was long before they had computers. "Let's see," the lady said, finally getting my information and work record. She pulled out the appropriate papers and examined them. "Says here that you worked too many hours for partial unemployment."

"Well, it was worth a try," I answered dejectedly, then turned to go.

"I'm sorry," she continued without raising her head or voice. "It will have to be full benefits instead."

"What?" I exclaimed, turning back to her.

"Yup. Full unemployment. No doubt about it."

She was serious. I didn't argue anymore. It was more than I had expected. That winter, Edie, Josh, and I lived like royalty.

6

GETTING INTO MEDICAL SCHOOL

I n the spring of 1975, I went with Dominic on a canoe trip through the cranberry bogs of the Pine Barrens in South Jersey, where our physics teacher lived.

The Pine Barrens was truly a land time forgot. At that time, I had lived in New Jersey most of my life and had never heard of them. I fell in love with the quiet, peaceful rivers that flowed through it, its iron-tinged water, and its slow pace of life.

On another trip, we visited Doctor Halley, who loved the Pine Barrens. He was the image of a professor - bespectacled, hair like Albert Einstein, and untidy. Doctor Halley was more than happy to show us around.

"Do you know where the rebels got their cannonballs in the American Revolution?" he asked.

Both of us shook our heads.

"Right here," he said proudly. "The iron was carried to Valley Forge on America's first two-lane highway."

Then Doctor Halley pointed out some huge mounds.

"Do you know what they are?" he asked.

We both shook our heads.

"They're Indian burial monuments made out of shells. When they decay, they become lime. That's where the early settlers got their lime from."

We stopped in a museum that memorialized the Pine Barrens. He even showed us a few cranberry bogs.

Someday, I'll write a book about it. [1]

Then, the papers arrived for an interview in Newark and a second at Rutgers. I was excited, never having been to one before, but I was confident, too. After all, I'd spent three and a half years with the farm workers.

Compared to that, this is a piece of cake!

At Newark, a black doctor asked me, "Why do you want to be a doctor?"

With my eyes downcast, I replied, "I want to help people. I've been on the farms of America. It's a nightmare. Tuberculosis, polio, smallpox – things that are supposed to be gone in America – are raging among the farmworkers ..." For a moment, I thought I was back on the boycott.

I looked up, and the doctor was crying. At the time, I knew I was in.

" ... All I want is to improve their access to good care."

GOD must have been listening, too. I meant every word of it. I momentarily forgot about getting into medical school and just told the truth.

Then it was on to Rutgers for my second interview. A student examined me.

They didn't even think enough of me to have one of the faculty do the interview.

"You might be number one hundred-ten this year among the applicants," she explained, "and only one hundred-eight will be accepted. If you reapply next year, the admission team will consider that and place you below the cut-off."

Guess this year, I'm out.

"Let's get started," she said matter-of-factly. "As I see it, the most important question is 'Why do you care?'"

Well, I got nothing to lose. Better just be honest.

"I guess it's because of my parents. They loved me when they didn't have to. I just want to pass it along."

"A little idealistic, don't you think?"

"Maybe. My parents are saintly people. My Uncle Ray often calls my mother 'Saint Ellen.' She had to be to put up with all us kids. Once I asked her how I could ever repay her. She said, 'By giving to others.' Pretty simple but true. I've lived that way ever since."

The interview went well after that, as we talked about my childhood experiences through college. She laughed at some and coaxed me into being just myself.

I also applied to seven out-of-state schools but never received an interview that year. I guess the reciprocity, or lack thereof, between states came into play.

I received word in the mail that I was accepted to medical school, first at Newark, then at Rutgers. I was surprised I was approved there; I expected a rejection. It shows you how much I knew. GOD watched over me even then.

I needed to choose, but the pick was easy.

I've had enough of city life. It's no place to raise a family.

So, I chose Rutgers. The college was in rural Piscataway. It was, to me, a country setting with grass, trees, and a golf course. I could attend school there and live nearby with my burgeoning family.

In the meantime, Edie was working in the office for the farm workers again. She took Josh with her. I also expected to work for them once I completed my residency. So, what if I'd be thirty-two when I finished residency? That didn't bother me. After all, I would be thirty-two someday anyway, right?

7

VAL AGAIN

I tried to get in touch with Jimmy Hokey, but every time I tried, Danny or his sister said he wasn't home. I left a number, but he never called back. Ever since he'd returned from Vietnam, he was a different person. After a few rebuffs, I didn't call anymore.

Then one night, I had an idea, *If she's still with him, Val could be my go-between.*

But it's been years, the good voice insisted.

The fact that I loved her didn't stop me. However, as it's said, "There is no greater fool than he that believes his own lies."

I'm only going to find out about Jimmy.

Yeah, right.

I went to her old house where her mother opened the door.

She had been laughing with Val until she saw me standing there. Her laughter stopped, and she looked at me with a frown.

"What are *you* doing here?" she asked behind a half-opened door.

"I've come to talk with Valerie."

"Let sleeping dogs lie."

Val was inside listening. "Let him in," she said.

I entered. We sat uncomfortably across from each other. Val was dressed sexy in her trademark blue blouse and cut-off jeans, prominently displaying her long, tanned legs. I tried not to look at them, but my eyes involuntarily kept returning. She was a woman now and had filled in all the places that needed it. She was shapely all over with a body that would've tempted Gandhi.

Maybe this wasn't such a good idea.

"Why did you come?" her mother asked tersely.

"Came to see if Val knew anything about Jimmy."

"I haven't seen him in years," Val replied.

"Why not?"

Val blushed. "I'm married to George now."

"George? Do I know him?"

"No." Then abruptly changing the subject, she asked, "How are you?"

"Couldn't be better. If I felt any better, there'd be two of me."

Val giggled, and her mother shot her a disapproving glance.

"You're looking good," she said.

"Thanks. You are, too."

I was keenly aware of her mother's presence.

Finally, Val rose and said, "I have errands to run. Want to come along?"

Against my better judgment, I replied, "Yeah."

"Just be back in an hour," her mother said brusquely. "I need the car to pick Dawn[1] up at school." As we left, her mother whispered to me, "Don't try anything funny."

Val and I got in the car. She took off, and we went toward the grocery store in the opposite direction from Hershung Park.

Remember what happened the last time, a good voice reminded me.

Go ahead. You're both grown-ups now, an evil voice told me.

Whew! Want to be alone with her, but not that alone.

Val interrupted the stillness. "Boy, am I glad to be out of that house,"

"Seems like old times."

"In many ways, it's still the same."

I didn't know what she meant, so I remained quiet for once.

"I got married May 6th, 1972," she said, driving toward the store.

"That's funny. So, did I."

"I know."

"How—" I stopped mid-sentence, realizing where this question would lead. Honestly, I was happy that Val cared enough to look in the local paper and remember me. At the same time, I was frightened.

Then I remembered my stated reason for coming.

"If you don't mind me asking, what happened with you and Jimmy?"

"No, I don't mind telling you about it. The jerk actually asked me if we were in a boat and our child and him fell in the water, which one would I save?"

"How'd you answer?"

"Said I didn't know. Jimmy wanted me to say him because we could always make another child. What a jerk. I'm glad I never had any kids by him."

We were silent for a moment, then she continued, "Speaking of children, I have a daughter named Amy. Her delivery was hard. Over twenty-four hours. But it was worth it. She makes me laugh."

"I have a son, Josh, and I know what you mean."

We stopped at the grocery store. Valerie went right to the produce aisle like she had a purpose. She picked out a bunch of bananas and grapes before squeezing the melons.

"This one's not ripe yet, but this one is," she explained.

We then continued to talk about our children.

That's safe.

Before we knew it, Val had finished, and we headed back to the car.

Came to straighten some things out. They're more crooked than ever.

Once inside the car, she asked abruptly. "Wanna go to the park?"

Get out now! The good voice said.

What's the matter? You scared? Came the bad voice.

"Thought your mother needed the car."

"George, my husband, dropped me off this morning before work. I've been stranded with the witch since then."

"Oh, c'mon. It can't be that bad. She *is* babysitting. You left Amy with her."

Then we became silent again. Val pulled away and went back toward her mother's. The tension was so thick you could feel it.

We finally pulled into her driveway.

"I'll see you sometime," I said nervously.

"Sure."

8

MOVING FOR MEDICAL SCHOOL

I left with Edie and our son for New Brunswick (close to the school) in the summer of 1975. Edie worked for the farm workers again, and they needed someone to occupy the two-story union house.

We planned that I bike to school, thereby staying in shape, while Edie would use the car when she needed it.

It may have worked, too, except for thieves. On the night of August 24, 1975, when I was on the first floor watching the Mets get a no-hitter pitched against them by Ed Halicki[1], I heard a noise in the bathroom upstairs—the fire escape attached to its window. Edie was in the kitchen near me, but Josh was asleep in his second-floor room. I started to sweat. It struck me that I was not just the provider for my family. Also, I was their protector.

I went to the steps. I shouted, "Take anything, but leave my son alone! I will stay here!"

After a while, I climbed the stairs carrying a hammer as a weapon.

This is not a good time to talk about nonviolence.

Edie followed closely behind me. We saw two sets of footprints in the bathtub. It was a good thing that I had stayed downstairs.

They might've killed me if I had stumbled on them.

GOD knew what HE was doing.

Edie and I went to make sure Josh was safe. He slept without a care in the world. The thieves had left him alone.

We continued to our room. Edie looked around and noted, "Everything they took was already broken."

"Why'd you keep it then?" I asked.

Edie shrugged and continued, "Maybe when they learn that they don't work, they'll get angry and come back."

"Let me get this straight. They removed junk. As I see it, they did us a favor."

"You would."

"Now, what's that supposed to mean?"

Edie just shrugged again. I continued, "At any rate, they're certainly not pros. We were in the house! We could've run into them. Probably on drugs. There's no telling what they'll do."

The next day, I boarded the windows to the fire escape. No one was going to invade our house again!

This is no way to live!

Fear is crippling, worse than being beaten or even death.

The next night, Wayne Rutley and Lisa Noel came over for dinner.

"There's no room for us at either of our homes," Wayne complained. "What do you think if you shared a house with us?"

"That might work," I thought of getting my family away from the thieves. Besides, because of my experience with the farm workers union, I was an expert in communal living. Wayne was studying law and couldn't afford his own house.

Edie and I moved again, this time to Bridgewater. The large two-storied country house had three bedrooms, one and a half baths, and a basement suitable for my studying. I waited for school to start.

Finally, it did. Entering medical school was scary for me. I was with students from Ivy League Schools. However, I was just somebody trying to get along. I wore a chip on my shoulder to prove to them that I belonged.

I discovered an indoor basketball court there.

Don't know how, but I'm gonna get on it.

Over a hundred students packed the lectures. You screamed to ask a question. The yelling served two purposes. One was to be heard, and the other was to get the instructor's attention.

This ain't for me.

A student taped each lecture. Different people were responsible for transcribing each lesson, so we had legible notes for all topics presented. The school owned a mimeograph machine[2], which I knew how to use from working with the farm workers union. The other students didn't.

"Look, you need a printer[3] familiar with the mimeograph machine. Otherwise, it could get broken," I told the school administrators.

They eventually agreed and chose me as the printer. I collected the typewritten notes, mimeographed them, and distributed them. Soon, I didn't attend lecture hall but shot hoops in the gym instead.

Then, I realized, *Monday through Friday is not enough time to dissect the cadaver. Have to work on the weekends too to get some things done.*

When an extensive dissection occurred, several students shared the body, combining two tables. When the skull needed to be opened, the others became queasy.

"Give me the drill," I said with bravado.

I'll show those Ivy Leaguers how it's done.

So, I took the drill and exposed the brain, thinking I was striking a blow for the little guy. It shows you how stupid I was. GOD didn't let me get sick, and for that, I'm grateful.

In the Physiology lab, I argued with the instructor about using mice for experiments. "Wouldn't a film be enough?"

"No!" she refuted my protests. "You must see it."

"Why? So, the mice have to die a painful death?"

"I don't think you can appreciate it any other way."

"That's bull!" I stormed.

She slammed down her notebook on a countertop. "Listen! It's how we do it and so will you!"

She was a professor, and I was a student. The experiment went ahead as planned.

The papers from the note-taking service, which I was now in charge of, needed to be available before the tests. So, I hired a tempestuous apprentice named Rick Hernandez. He had a short fuse that earned him the nickname of "firecracker." However, Rick was the best person you could want to know between explosions. He was from Fifty-ninth Street, in the same block as Dominic, via Cuba. We became good friends.

We started a basketball league. I wanted Rick on my team. That started a minor brouhaha.

The blacks wanted their own team. One of them, John Fontana, was excellent. Because the court was small, John could shoot as soon as the ball came in.

Six-foot-five Alan Kellen and Larry Sawyer, who was also over six feet, were on my team, which was good too.

The first year dragged on with its tedious and time-consuming labs. The Bakke case was prominent in the news then and diverted the student's attention. He was refused admission to medical school because Bakke was thirty-two years old. He sued, protesting that the rejection was because of his white color.

I had mixed feelings about it. On the one hand, I saw what affirmative action and quotas could do. It was supposed to ensure that the inner city would have doctors when the students returned. However, the Blacks in our college were not from New Jersey. The Black students with good grades were off at Harvard or Texas, not Rutgers. The university tapped other sources to fulfill the quota. They even had an African prince. I doubt he would set foot in the inner city, let alone practice there.

However, affirmative action also increased class size. Rutgers was a small medical school with student numbers in the teens before the state money. Along with affirmative action, the number ballooned to around a hundred. That way, the state school could accommodate the twenty percent Black students and still be eighty percent White. In effect, the White student population went from teens to eighty. I would not have been accepted into medical school if it weren't for that. So, I was caught in the middle. I just wanted justice done.

I thought the answer to any problem was on the basketball court. Instead of the lecture hall, where I couldn't ask questions anyway, and I had type-written notes, I shot hoops. It kept me in shape and cleared my mind. As a result, we won the basketball title. White men can jump! Isn't it good to know that your doctor can play basketball?

9

THE PHONE CALL

One night, I received the phone rang at 4:00 in the morning. Edie poked me to answer it.

"Hello?" I answered sleepily.

"Are you doing anything?" my brother, Johnny, asked.

"I *was* sleeping."

Ignoring the sarcasm in my voice, he continued, "It's only 1:00 here."

"Where are you now?"

"In Albuquerque."

"New Mexico?"

"Last I looked."

"Well, it must be something important to call at this hour. Is anybody sick?"

"No, I'm okay. So is everybody else as far as I know."

"Then why'd you call?" I asked, fully awake now.

"Couldn't sleep."

"You called *me* at four in the morning to tell me *you* couldn't sleep!" I barked.

Edie, lying beside me, turned over. "Who is it?"

I cupped my hand over the receiver and whispered, "Johnny. Go back to sleep."

"And why can't you get to sleep?" I asked against my better judgment.

"I've had such an unforgettable day. I had to tell someone about it."

"Well, go ahead."

"I went to interview for a math teacher's job in New Mexico." Johnny taught math at a technical school in Passaic, New Jersey, for a couple of years. This was a chance to get out a little and see the world— at least, the US.

"That's great news!"

"Thought you might like it." And then Johnny related this story. "A friend of mine told me about an opportunity there. I was burned out at Passaic Tech[1], so I went. Sort of gave me a chance to see the southwest. We didn't see it all in '69. Carlsbad Caverns was spectacular. So was the White Sands. Anyway, I was in Albuquerque sharing an apartment with some lady. She was crazy."

"And you're not?"

Ignoring me, he said, "You know me. I only own one suit. I had an interview for a math teacher position in Los Alamos. It's a dream job. Most of the parents have PhDs."

"You know what we call them in medical school?" I interrupted, forgetting the time.

"What?"

"A BS is bull*#*#, an MS is more *#*#, and a PhD is piled high and deep."

When he stopped laughing, he said, "Anyway. I had to wear my only suit to the interview. On the way there, I became low on gas and stopped. In New Jersey, there's always an attendant to pump gas. Not in New Mexico. There you pump it yourself. So, I did. At least, I tried.

"I got out and pumped the gas, but I spilled a good amount on my suit.

"Driving to Los Alamos, it stunk. I opened all the windows, hoping the air would evaporate the gas smell.

"When I got to Los Alamos, the principal insisted on interviewing me.

"He sniffed. 'Do you smell gas?'

"'No,'" I lied. Of course, I smelt it! I was wearing it!

"'Must be coming from construction workers outside,'" the principal said.

"He rose from his desk to close the windows. The smell got worse.

"Then, the principal took out a cigar and was about to light it when I jumped up. 'Don't light that match!' I screamed. Well, now I had to tell him the whole story.

"'That's a good one!' the principal laughed. He told everyone in the school, and I got the job."

I laughed. Yes, it was a good one, even at four in the morning.

Edie rolled over and asked, "What are you laughing at?"

Again, I cupped my hand over the receiver.

"The shenanigans of my brother," I whispered. "Tell you about them at breakfast."

She went back to sleep. I did, too, after finally getting off the phone with Johnny.

10

THE SHELTER

Eddie went to work because finances at home were tight. I thought it was temporary. Everything turned out quite differently. Her job was at a youth shelter, placing disturbed kids. She met Vicki Gurki, a fellow worker. Wayne and Sue Durban were the house parents who lived there permanently. Sue had a son, Jonathan, from a previous marriage, who was a year older than Josh. They became good buddies.

At the Christmas party of that year, 1975, I met one of The Shelter Kids, fifteen-year-old Jimmy. We immediately hit it off. He was ten years my junior and looked up to me as a big brother. He loved card games and was always teaching me new ones. Spades, Hearts, Whist, Canasta–you name it, Jimmy knew it.

At first, I didn't want Edie to work because that meant I was not providing for her and Josh. We had words about it many times.

"As I see it," she'd say, "you could quit school, get a job, and we lose any chance of getting a better future."

I hated to admit it, but she was right. I couldn't argue.

"I'm more than willing to make a little sacrifice now, for a hope that tomorrow it will be worth it," Edie would say.

What could I say to that?

"Besides, I like working at The Shelter," she continued. "Those kids need me."

When we started, I thought she would follow my lead. How was I to know I would follow hers?

Shortly after, the director left, and Vicki became the new director. The Shelter moved to a temporary house but needed a permanent home. Over the summer of 1976, I looked for work and took a job running recreation at The Shelter. Now I would get paid for playing basketball! I thought I was in Heaven!

My job differed from everyone's because SETA[1], a government agency, funded me. I worked at The Shelter under the new director, but SETA controlled the purse strings in Trenton.

Vicki liked to play basketball and challenged me to games. She was around six feet tall and a starter on her college team. No offense to women who play, but Vicki couldn't keep up with me. Maybe, she liked to lose.

Vicki asked, "Can you ump games in my women's softball league?"
I need the cash.
"How much?" I asked.
"Five bucks for first base and ten for behind the plate."
Not bad. I know the rules. How hard can it be?

So, we settled it. In one game, Vicki's team played the prison team. Suspiciously, the other umpire, always behind the plate, called in sick. So, I worked behind the plate—something I'd never done before—and called the game by myself. The prison team took the field first. When the pitcher hurled the first pitch, it was fast, and I thought it might hit me. So, I ducked.

"Stree-ike!" I called, again upright.

The pitcher threw the ball so hard that it must have gone over the plate. Besides, it's against the prison team. Who wants to argue with them?

"Ump, you need glasses," the batter hissed under her breath, not looking at me.

I acted like I hadn't heard and let the matter drop.

Meanwhile, I worked nights or weekends at "The Shelter," as we called it. The children became "Shelter Kids." In this age of political correctness, perhaps we wouldn't call them that today. But we did then. They were all teenagers from broken families, except one girl whose father was sick. All of us tried to give them love. That's what they needed, not jail.

But, no one wanted them. The neighbors always found some excuse to keep us out. In a way, I can't blame them. The noise, the increased traffic—who wants a bunch of teenagers living next to them? However, where could they go? They weren't juvenile delinquents.

Then, we found a place. It had a big yard that the kids could play in. The house had two sections with an apartment in front where the Durbans could live. Behind their quarters was a classroom, a dining room, a big kitchen, and a living room. In the back, outside was a screened-in area forty by thirty for picnics and, of course, water fights.

Upstairs were four bedrooms off a long hall. On the left of the stairs was a smaller TV room. I spent many an hour there in the wee hours of the morning watching the hallway to ensure there was no hanky-panky between boys and girls. Next to it, at the top of the stairs, was a bathroom. The fire escape was outside one of the females' bedroom windows.

Before the neighbors could interfere, we rented the place and moved in.

With my medical background, I became responsible for teaching birth control to the kids.

"You take birth control pills each day for one month," I began one summer day in the classroom.

A hand in the back shot up, "Ya' mean ya' don't put 'em in?"

"Put them in? Where?"

"Ya' know, down below on the night you have sex."

This ain't gonna be easy.

For recreation, I took them on hikes to state parks. On one, I invented a story. "It was right here," I said, standing at the top of a cliff. "I had the kids out hiking, like today. One of them fell over the cliff and lost his arm. A claw replaced it. We called him 'Jack the Claw.'"

"Oh, c'mon," someone snorted.

"Really! I swear."

However, I had sown the seed. When a stranger stopped by the mailbox for a moment one day, I exclaimed, "It's him! It's 'Jack the Claw'!"

It didn't matter who he was. Wayne Durban and I couldn't let an opportunity slip by to insist it was 'Jack the Claw.' Whenever something was missing, we blamed it on him.

Wayne and I rigged up a hanger on the girls' window, a string tied to the bottom. We attached the free end of the string to the bathroom window. The hanger clattered against the window of the girls' bedroom by pulling on it. We remained unseen.

One night as the young ladies were going to bed, I went into the bathroom, tugged the string, and it rattled the hanger against their window.

"What was that?" they screamed.

"It's 'Jack the Claw' on the fire escape!" I shouted.

More screams.

On the first floor, Wayne clanged noisily up the fire escape and ripped off the hanger. "Just saw a man running away. Think it was 'Jack the Claw.'"

There was no sleep that night.

Then there was the big, blue van we used to cart the kids around. One Saturday night in February, I took the kids to a play. On the way back, I was late, so I took a shortcut through the Duke Estate animal sanctuary.

That's odd. The bushes moved.

The kids were all asleep. So, I stopped the van. The bushes stopped, too.

Must be my imagination.

I started again. The bushes moved again.

What's going on?

My curiosity was piqued, and I parked and emerged from the vehicle. There were hundreds of hoofprints in the snow.

Deer? Where?

As I neared, I realized they weren't bushes but antlers! I had stumbled upon a herd of deer, maybe a couple hundred. I was a goner if they spooked in any way or ran at me. I respectfully retraced my steps silently in the snow.

Another time, I wanted to remove my desk from my parent's house. I needed the van and some boys to get it, but if I informed my mother too early, she would cook a meal for all of us. I didn't want that, so I waited until we were ready to leave, giving her about a half-hour notice.

"Mom, this is Joseph. I'm coming with six kids to get my desk. Don't cook."

Mom sat at the dining room table across from Dad when I walked through the door. Between them on the table was a plate of twenty-five hamburgers!

"We were just sitting down for lunch," she smiled. "Do you want to join us?"

I still don't know how Mom did it with that tiny kitchen. I threw up my hands in surrender.

11

TWO MORE BOYS

L iving with Wayne Rutley and Lisa Noel didn't work. Nobody's fault, just two couples with different agendas. Edie and I moved to an apartment nearby in Somerville.

The three-bedroom garage-less apartment was the second story of a house: not as big as the last house, but the apartment was adequate. A stairway was inside in the front, and a spiral one in the back. I could study in a tiny attic cubicle.

We lived around the corner from Somerset hospital. I volunteered in the family clinic that summer. I even wrote an article about patient satisfaction (or dissatisfaction, depending upon your point of view). The apartment was closer to school, and The Shelter, with a Carvel ice cream stand nearby. That convinced me. However, I was still a commuter.

An office building stood next door. Whenever I locked myself out, I often climbed the tree between it and our living quarters and jumped off the tree onto the roof of the second story. I opened the window, and *voila*, I was in the kitchen! Easy, wasn't it? Mountain climbing came in handy.

Once I was in McDonald's with Josh (nearly four) and Johnathan.

We were at our own table. With his mouth nearly full of hamburger, he asked me, "Daddy, where do boys and girls come from?"

Oh, no. The dreaded question. Might as well tell him before someone else does. He'll probably forget about it tomorrow. Don't make it a big deal. Use your medical knowledge to explain the "birds and bees," and cloud the facts.

With my face reddening a wee bit, I said, "Boys have a penis and girls a vagina. The boy puts his penis in the girl's vagina. And she gets pregnant. After nine months, a baby comes out."

The McDonald's had become busy. It seemed like people were everywhere. I ended my explanation in a whisper. I'll never forget what happened next.

Josh gets up and yells, "You mean girls' have vaginas and boys' have penises!"

Everybody there turned toward me like I was a pervert. Nobody said a word. I just wanted to crawl into a hole and disappear. With as much dignity as I could muster, we left. Oh, the joys of being a parent.

Edie was pregnant when we moved. Then on October 29, in the middle of the early morning, she went into labor before it was light out. I determined that this delivery would be different from the first, and I would be present.

"Blow in and blow out," I said calmly.

"You blow in and blow out, you *#*#."

"That was uncalled for."

"I'll tell you what's uncalled—Ooh! Ooh!"

I had to act fast. We put on some clothes and then sped to the hospital.

"Wait here!" the nurse said, pointing to the empty waiting room. She wheeled the nearly crazed Edie back.

The seconds inched by slowly.

What's going on?

In half an hour, the nurse returned.

"You're a daddy again."

"Is everybody okay?"

She nodded.

"Is the baby a boy or a girl?"

"A boy. Do you have a name picked out?"

"Jeremiah."

And so, it was. Now, we had two boys.

Months later—the following summer, when Jeremiah was learning how to walk and get into things, we all went to the Red Shanty reunion —a yearly gathering of friends in the country. We played volleyball, and I enjoyed the game. Jeremiah's little ball accidentally went below the sandbox. He tried to retrieve it, but it rolled next to a beehive.

As a father, I couldn't let him go near it, could I? My reaction was to lift him, and the bees stung me before I had a chance to think. I demand the line of Hamlet is read, "To bee, or not to bee."

Jeremiah escaped injury while my legs ballooned. Thank the Lord I'm not allergic to bees.

Wonder if any of them are allergic to us?

Then Jimmy, one of The Shelter Kids, was placed in a group home. He hated it and ran away. One early morning, I discovered him asleep on our front stairs.

"Where are you going?" I was half-asleep, too.

Awakening, he yawned, "Greenwich Village."

"Why don't you come in here?"

He did and gladly never left.

Now, we had three boys.

And his name begins with "J." He'll fit right in.

Edie and I put Jimmy in a special high school for his senior year. Sometimes, he would lock himself out and climb up the tree beside our apartment, as I did.

Jimmy often sat on the County Courthouse steps whenever it was sunny. One time, the police brought him home for smoking marijuana. Another time, he held up placards from one to ten whenever women passed. Jimmy was not too bright.

"What are you doing?" I stormed.

"It was meant as a joke."

"This is not some Olympics!" I slammed his door.

That winter, I took him and his friend to the frozen waterfalls at Child's State Park in Pennsylvania. On the way home, a state trooper stopped our car because it looked suspicious to him.

The policeman asked Jimmy, who was not driving, "Do you have any ID?"

An average person would answer, "No, I don't."

Not he. Jimmy removed a picture from his wallet with no printing on it and pointed to it, "That's me."

The next thing I knew, I was spread-eagled with my arms on the car's roof while the Statey frisked me. I never took Jimmy to the park again.

That was the winter of 1977-78, with its three big snowstorms. For the second and third, I was stranded and slept at the hospital for a few days. Residents skied to work. The entrance ramps were plowed on the highways but not the exits. You could enter but not exit. Entire cities were closed.

We built an igloo in our backyard for all three boys and used it as a slide. I poured water on the igloo to convert the snow into ice. It lasted all winter.

One morning, Edie had to go to work. I shoveled the driveway, but the plow came by and blocked her in with new snow.

"A little snow ain't gonna stop me," she said.

"Wait—"

However, she gunned the engine of the Nova and went through anyway. It was like going through a ring of fire at a circus. The white powder went everywhere. The starter came off, but Edie drove on.

JIMMY GRADUATED FROM HIGH SCHOOL. I don't know how he did it, maybe with smoke and mirrors. After graduation, Jimmy moved to California but couldn't keep a job there.

12

LARRY HAWLEY

I juggled being a husband and father with medical school, trying to keep the two lives separate. If not one, then the other would rear its head. It wasn't easy for either Edie or me. We were always busy. I have to say; she put me through school.

In between the second and third years, during the summer of 1977, Edie and I took Josh and the still-crawling Jeremiah and went to Bear Mountain in upstate New York. Larry Hawley, his wife, Kathy, and their daughter, Jessica (three) met us there. We rented two cabins by a lake. A mother, and her five-year-old son, Byron, occupied the next cabin.

Being a mischievous person, I thought, *I'll fool the kids.*

I taped gumdrops to a tree deep in the forest, out of sight of the cabins. My father had done something similar to me when I was a boy.

Cupping my hand next to my ear, I claimed, "I just heard a squirrel speak."

"Oh? C'mon," Josh said with the skeptical Byron at his side. "Squirrels don't talk."

"Oh, yeah. This one did. Must be a leprechaun," I continued rubbing my chin between my forefinger and thumb as if deep in thought. "He told me there was a gumdrop tree to be found."

Josh and Byron, no longer skeptics, ran into the forest to find the candy. They saw the tape glistening and ran to the tree. They began to stuff their mouths with gumdrops.

"You have to plant one for next year!" I called.

They did it quickly and then ate the remainder.

That oughtta' keep 'em happy.

The next day, Larry took Josh and me with his little daughter out in a rented boat on the lake. Watching him play with his beard when he wasn't rowing around the peaceful lake was fun. What a beautiful place!

Larry had a temper. He related this story while we rowed around the lake.

"I was driving once along a divided highway with Kathy in the passenger seat and Jessica in the back. It was winter, so I was wearing a ski mask. Kathy and I fought. Something about directions and getting lost. I got so mad at her that I pulled off the road onto the shoulder. When I did, I threw my ski mask at her, crossed over the highway divider, and hitchhiked the other way. Kathy didn't wait long but took off with the car.

"Soon, someone stopped to pick me up. A while later, a police car pulls in front of us with sirens blaring, motioning us to pull over. Another police car shows up behind us, blocking any chance of us turning around. I wondered what the driver did.

"Get out of the car now! And put your hands up!" a cop yelled.

So, we did. I thought this guy must be a real wise guy.

Then the cop asked, "Why did you throw your ski mask away?"

"What?"

"Someone just robbed the bank. We thought you did it."

I started to laugh.

"And what are you laughing at?" one cop asked.

"What kind of a bank robber hitchhikes for a getaway?"

"A stupid one. Maybe you."

"Oh brother."

I explained about the fight with Kathy. They let us get back in the car. After a few miles, I noticed that the driver was trembling. He pulled off the highway again and said, "Get out! I never want to see you again!"

I rocked the boat with laughter.

13

VAL AGAIN, AGAIN

The following summer of 1978, I had a few days off, so I arranged to see Val at her apartment. Who knows why I kept going back? Perhaps I liked misery.

"I almost died from a burst appendix," she confessed after we exchanged a few pleasantries. Flabbergasted, I didn't know what to say.

"I have another child, Matt," she continued. "He's in the playpen, now."

"That's funny. I have two more boys. Jimmy and Jeremiah. Jimmy is a foster child who we're putting through high school."

I followed her into another room, where we saw a boy asleep in a playpen.

"That's Matt," she whispered.

"Adorable," I said.

Why am I not the father?

She and I went together to the basement for something. We were alone. Val was beautiful in her cut-off jeans again and blue blouse.

Think it's the same pair she had last time.

She dropped something and bent over to pick it up. I gulped. I almost took her in my arms and kissed her.

What am I doing? Have to get outta here.

Oh, Satan was having a field day that day! So was my flesh!

"George is working late," she said. "Why don't you stay for dinner?"

"Okay, but then I have to go."

She smiled and cooked some spaghetti.

I didn't know then I would not see her again for fourteen years.

14

MORE MEDICAL SCHOOL

Meanwhile, Dominic stayed in pre-med at William Paterson. He debated whether to go to osteopathic school or to become an M.D. Dominic described the interview to me at the osteopathic school in Philadelphia.

"Do you speak Spanish?" The interviewer asked as he examined his credentials.

"Yes."

"You're in."

So much for his becoming an M.D.

Then, in my sophomore year, I no longer had a chip on my shoulder and was just another student who wanted to pass.

I remained in charge of the note-taking service. That year, I didn't attend a single lecture; it wasted precious time. But I read diligently. I took the school tests and passed with high grades, buttressing my habit of not attending lectures.

My parents gave us a Dodge Swinger. Edie drove to work in the Nova, and I went to school in the Dodge. Josh rode with me to the Day Care Center while she took Jeremiah.

On our way there, I taught Josh the alphabet. "'F' for fence."

"F-fence," he replied from his car seat.

It was *fun* to see Josh progress.

The government tested our medical knowledge three times. The first exam lasted two days following the second year in 1977. I prepared for it all year. I passed, then entered the third year, a hospital practical experience.

They called us "Roads Scholars" because Rutgers didn't have a teaching hospital. The students commuted to a hospital, where the instructor lectured us after we saw the patients. It influenced our second year when we had to choose where to go for each rotation (Medicine, Surgery, Pediatrics, Gynecology, and Psychiatry). Each hospital was noted for something different. I needed a partner and chose Rick Hernandez.

IN MY THIRD YEAR, I drove to the hospitals. It was a whole new experience for me. The first rotation was Internal Medicine. I was to spend six weeks at Raritan Hospital and then at Hunterdon Hospital for another six.

My first upper-level resident was a short guy called Dr. Ming. He was half Chinese but spoke perfect English. I stuck out my hand to greet him with a handshake. He turned the other way.

Perhaps he didn't see me.

"I'm your new student," I said.

He laughed.

"What's so funny?"

"Your accent. When we see patients, maybe you should be quiet."

"Wait a minute. No one ever mentioned my accent before."

"Well, *I* am. Be quiet."

I was fuming. Dr. Ming wasn't just making fun of me, but he was denigrating my parents, too, both of whom came from Brooklyn. However, he was my upper-level resident for six weeks.

I should be quiet. Maybe it'll get better.

It didn't.

There was only one intern, Don Black, that was down-to-earth. Unfortunately, he fell asleep while driving home after being on-call at the hospital for a long night. The surgeon amputated his leg to save his life.

No one had ever explained to me the grueling hours we kept.

Then, one morning, Dr. Ming said to me, "Thek, prepare a briefing of Mr. Downs for tomorrow morning."

I worked all that night, going over the chart several times.

Show 'em what I can do.

Edie was very supportive.

The following day, I got up and presented the case.

"Mr. Downs is a fifty-year-old man … " and continued. I thought my presentation was flawless.

Dr. Ming smiled sarcastically. "Is that the way they taught you how to present a patient?"

"Why, yes," I answered, stunned.

"First of all, Mr. Downs is fifty-one. Your presentation treats facts as if they were unimportant."

"But it says right on the chart that he is fifty."

"If you were more careful, you would have noticed that yesterday was his birthday. And that accent, where did you get that, on some street corner?"

Petty! He set me up! If this is what it's like, I should quit.

This ain't for me, I thought as I drove home.

But Edie met me at the door.

"How'd it go?" she asked.

"Don't ask."

She became quiet. The phone rang. It was Rick Hernandez.

I explained to him what had happened.

"What are you gonna do?" he asked.

"Quit."

"Whoa! After all the years of hard work?"

I started to waver.

"It's only six weeks," he continued. "Give Hunterdon a try. It may be different."

"Okay. But if it's the same, I'm gone."

After those six trying weeks, I went to Hunterdon.

It was more laid back and more my style. I fit in better there.

This ain't so bad. Guess I'll see it through. Ming is the oddball.

Construction on hospitals is not like houses. They built parts at different times. We took a shortcut across the intervening roof to go from one tower to the other. It was like a deck on a ship, flat, easy to walk on, but high above the ground.

That winter was a turning point for me. Hunterdon was like an oasis in the desert. The residents and doctors were friendly. I did my rotations for six weeks of medicine and surgery (the other six were at Raritan) there, as well as eight weeks both of gynecology and psychiatry. The twelve weeks of Pediatrics at Muhlenberg with Dr. Palore completed my third year.

During the gynecological rotation at Hunterdon, I lost my wedding ring while scrubbing for surgery. I lathered my arms, removed the ring, put it in the greens I wore, and then forgot about it.

After the surgery, I changed to my work clothes. The laundry took the greens. It was too late. By the time I remembered, the ring was gone. Maybe it was an omen.

Rick met a nurse at Hunterdon. She lived on a farm where we often ate lunch. Even the cows seemed to be friendlier there.

In the spring, Larry Hawley had a car accident and was paralyzed from the nipples down. His thoracic spine broke at the fourth vertebrae. He fractured his ankles, too. Larry would never use them again anyway, right? However, the doctors decided to repair the ankles in the morning after the accident. Why? I don't know. I read his chart.

During the night, he exclaimed, "I can't breathe!"

"It's nothing," the nurse said and ignored him.

Larry died.

I examined the initial chest x-ray in the basement by myself the next day.

"He had a hemothorax[1]!" I shouted to no one.

How many other errors were covered up both in his case and others?

"If they hadn't been so preoccupied with his broken ankles, they would have seen it!" I agonized.

Even as a third-year medical student, I saw that his chest had been filling with blood. It turned out that the Azygous[2] Vein was clipped when the thoracic spine broke.

His death could have been avoided!

To make matters worse, I knew it!

Thinking of Jessica, I urged Kathy, "You should sue them."

"Perhaps it's a blessing."

"But Larry was a cerebral person. Even if he never walked again, he was still valuable."

"It's a blessing," she repeated and never sued. Larry was a classic case of missing the forest for the trees.

The ER should have picked it up.

To my shame, I let the matter drop. I forgot about my farm worker days. Now, I wanted to be an ER Doc.

I'll prevent another Larry from happening.

In my last year in medical school, my rotations were in doctors' offices. One was ENT, in the office building next to my apartment.

"Say you look familiar," the secretary commented while I waited. Later, she exclaimed, "I've got it! You live next door, don't you?"

"I do. But how did you know?"

"Because I see you climbing the tree to get into the house."

So be good! A secretary may be watching! GOD always is. What a profound realization that is—omnipresent. It boggles the mind. We are never alone. Everything we do is known. But then, I was just climbing trees, ignorant of any secretary or *Anyone* watching me.

The match, where you did your residency, was like a lottery: one never knew where one was going. It occurred in the fourth year. It was similar to applying to medical school all over again. The student rated the hospitals they wanted to go to, and the hospitals did the same. The match chose where you went. Interviews followed.

There weren't any ER residency programs in New Jersey at the time; I chose to interview in Pennsylvania and Ohio. Edie is from Philadelphia, so, Pennsylvania looked good.

On one trip, I picked up two teens hitchhiking.

"Where are you going?" I asked as they climbed in.

"To the mall," one answered.

"It's cold," I noted. "Look, I don't need that coat back there, and you will. Please take it."

They did as they emerged. Then they vanished. When I glanced to see where they had gone, I didn't see them!

Where did they go? Maybe down a side road that I can't see from here.

Perhaps they weren't boys. I foolishly thought they were then, but now I think they were angels. Anyway, be careful to whom you offer rides. You never know who it might be.

15

JIMMY COMES HOME

Through the match, I was assigned a residency at Geisinger Medical Center in Danville, Pennsylvania. It was the one I wanted because Geisinger was like Hunterdon, laid back, and friendly. My ignorance would not be a joke there.

One night, near the end of medical school, the phone rang.

"Hello?"

It was Jimmy.

Lacking money, he'd been hitchhiking across America in March 1979.

"I'm stuck," a distraught Jimmy said hurriedly, without any pleasantries.

I was taken aback by how rapid-fire his speech was.

"Whoa! Slow down! Where are you?"

"I'm in this awful rain on Route 81 on the Virginia-Pennsylvania border. The guy I'm with is from France. Can you come and pick us up?"

"I'll be there as soon as possible, but it will be at least a couple hours."

As I hung up, I realized I didn't have a car that could make the trip.

I called Rick Hernandez.

"Can you come over?" I explained the situation. "I need a car."

Without hesitation, he answered, "Sure. Want some company?"

One problem was traveling through Harrisburg. Three Mile Island[1] had occurred then, and they had evacuated the area.

Rick and I went anyway, stopping for gas near Three Mile Island. There was no one at the pumps, and the station was closed.

"What do we do now?" he asked.

"Go until we find one open."

"We're almost on 'E' now. What happens if we run out of gas?"

"We turn into pumpkins? I don't know."

We were about to run out of gas when we found an open station. If we stuck our hands out the window, the radio probably would have played from the radiation.

Rick continued south on Route 81. When we saw the sign for Hagerstown, he exclaimed, "Wait a minute! There is no Pennsylvania-Virginia line!"

I examined the map. The two states don't border each other anywhere.

"Where is Jimmy? On the Virginia-West Virginia border or the Pennsylvania-Maryland line?" Rick questioned.

"I don't know. Keep driving. Maybe we'll find him."

"That's just great!" he replied angrily.

Rick and I passed the Maryland border: no Jimmy. We crossed the Maryland-West Virginia line; still no one. I visualized the smoke escaping from Rick's ears. He was like a firecracker. Then, it started to rain.

Good! It will douse him when he explodes.

The rain grew heavier. I saw a guy standing on the Virginia border, and Rick stopped. "Do you speak French?" I asked.

"*Oui.*"

"Get in."

We found Jimmy trying to keep warm in a dry donut shop.

"Well, it's about time you showed up," Jimmy complained. "You're very late. I was just about to give up on you."

I thought Rick would punch him.

Weeks later, after that adventure, he rented an apartment with a friend. Jimmy moved his things out of our house to his new place. He stayed in New Jersey when Edie and I moved to Pennsylvania. Distance separated us for a few months.

During that time, I wrote this song about him.

Rough Around the Edges

(Chorus)

He's rough around the edges
Guess he was raised that way,
But if nobody owns him
He's got no dues to pay.
He does not seem to know much
Doesn't have a lot to say,
He may be gone tomorrow
Sure, glad he's here today.

(Chorus)

He watches where he's going
But never looks behind
Can't tell what he's searching for
Or just what he will find.
Can't pin no labels on him
Guess he's one of a kind.
He's rough around the edges
But brings me peace of mind.
Sure, glad he's here today.

(Chorus)

He may not say the right thing
Whenever he's in a crowd.
He may not wear the right clothes
Might be a bit too loud.
But always full of laughter
Show you a real good time,
He's rough around the edges
And, *Lord, he's a friend of mine.

(Chorus)

AND WHEN THE angels call him
    To prepare to lay him down,
    His friends will try to see him
    They'll come from miles around.
    We'll sing the songs that he sang,
    Recalling him that way,
    Then we'll sing a eulogy
    And this is what we'll say.

(VARIATION OF CHORUS)

HE WAS rough around the edges
    Guess he was raised that way,
    But if nobody owned him
    He's had no dues to pay.
    He did not seem to know much

Didn't have a lot to say,
He may be gone tomorrow
Sure, glad of yesterday.

*Lord added later

16

GEISINGER

I graduated in May. Edie had to leave the Shelter. Three and a half years is a long time. She had Jeremiah at that time, and we rented the apartment. Edie wanted to stay. I would have liked to, but it was time to move on to Geisinger and residency. Every new beginning is also an ending.

So, we went to Geisinger. Before Johnny went to teach Air Force kids in Japan, he helped us with the move.

Edie and I lived in a house on the grounds at Geisinger, where I could take calls from home. There were eight houses in our unit. In the front was a big, shared, grassy area with trees along the side for the boys.

Bob Bagley, also a new emergency medicine resident, lived behind us. He ate off his murder-cycle, I mean motorcycle, in his kitchen.

"What are you doing?" I asked Bob the first day in the ER when he walked in on his hands.

"I want to show how flexible I am. My brother can do, it and he's an astronaut. I want to be like him."

"There has to be another way."

Later that morning, a patient arrived with a heart rhythm disturbance.

"I'm busy. Why don't you see him?" The attending physician, Mike Little, said.

Great! I'll show him what I can do.

I examined the patient, who was okay when I saw him.

No extra beats on his EKG or monitor. I'll order a digoxin level and discharge him. Will call him with the results.

Later that day, I asked Mike Little, "Say, how long does it take for a digitalis level to come back?"

"Digitalis or digoxin?" was his response.

Oops! I'd made a mistake. This wasn't medical school where attending physicians could quickly correct an error.

"He's not on digoxin but digitalis!" I exclaimed.

"Don't worry," Mike said, trying to calm me. "Digitalis breaks down to digoxin, and a level will work."

So, I waited until the next day when it was back.

The digoxin level returned high, so I called the patient. The daughter picked up the receiver.

"We would like to bring your father back," I began.

"So, would I. He went to Bingo last night and died."

I felt like dying too.

"Thanks for calling," she said.

She thinks I'm expressing my condolences. Maybe I should find a different line of work.

To whom could I admit my mistake? Not the family; they might sue.

Oh, the lawyers would have a field day with this. The very people I need to talk to, I can't. What a world!

But I refuse to be intimidated by lawyers. A good name for them is "bullies." One has to admit mistakes to be a good physician. A doctor is only human.

Should I stay or go?

Yes, I made errors, but I tried to improve the situation. I stayed. I didn't realize GOD was in control. I probably gave HIM a good laugh.

In my first year, I did rotations in medicine, surgery, pediatrics, orthopedics, and the ER.

There was a derogatory term, "Gomer," for abusers of the hospital. It stood for "Get Out of My Emergency Room."

I didn't like the term and thought it dehumanizing. It was like calling a black person N#*#*, a Jew a K#*, or an Italian a W#*. I guess there's one for every ethnic group. That kind of nonsense has no place in America. Whenever somebody applied that term, I took offense. I was an ombudsman, not an enemy.

I was on call every third night and every third weekend. We went from Friday night until Sunday afternoon. We made life and death decisions with no sleep. It was grueling. They had no IV team. We *were* the IV team. They called us "scut-boys" because we did the work nobody else would do.

When the call was due, it was for the whole hospital, including the units. The other residents nicknamed me "Black Cloud" because whenever I was on, disaster seemed to hit. It was better than, "007."

That first year of residency, that internship was demanding, especially when I was on call for surgery and internal medicine. When I was on rotations, they treated me as one of their residents—in other words, I took call regularly. That way, I knew the patients and why they were admitted.

I learned about the human body, both models (thank GOD, there are only two). I saw many patients and became a good resident. The ER saw everything except penetrating trauma. It lacked a knife and gun club. There is only so much you can learn from books. I needed hands-on experience as a teacher, too. More on that later.

One night, all the surgical residents were tired and sleeping. The attending surgeon walked me through an appendectomy. It was experience. We had an adage then; "See one, do one, teach one." We viewed everything as "experience." I did all right with the surgery. The patient lived.

We took call for the CCU and the ICU. The beds had a hole in them. I remember lying flat on my back while doing a lumbar puncture through that little hole. The patients were in a coma and weren't aware of what we were doing, and they didn't resist the needle. We did bone biopsies, burr holes, central lines, chest tubes, etc.—all for "experience."

Dr. Ross, the head of the ER, saw many patients at a time. In medical school, I cared for one case before I moved on to another. I was stuck in a linear mode. Simultaneously seeing many patients was new to me. However, it was a lot faster.

Dr. Ross loved to tell jokes and stories. One of them went back to when he was a resident. His wife had prepared a good meal and placed it on the table. "How is it?"

"I'm so tired. I could eat dog crap."

The next time he was on call, Dr. Ross came home to what he thought was a hamburger on a bun on his plate. When Dr. Ross ate it, something about the hamburger wasn't quite right. "What was that anyway?"

"Dog crap," his wife answered calmly.

He never claimed to be tired again.[1]

One of Dr. Ross' ideas was to have a departmental meeting every three months where all could air their complaints. It established the basis of a satisfied and happy ER. Taking care of the patients and their complaints was enough. We didn't need other problems.

One of the attending doctors was John Skinsiewski, which we shortened to just plain "Skins."

Skins took me aside one day and whispered, "When I was a resident here, I went out with Bob Norton from ophthalmology. We peed on some guy's lawn and got arrested."

"What?"

"Just don't let it happen to you," he continued softly.

"What? Peeing on someone's lawn or getting arrested?"

He never answered.

Skins loved to bowl. Our team from the ER included most of the attending physicians and some of the residents. It was a handicapped[2] league from the hospital and had fifteen teams.

Geisinger is in the middle of nowhere. We provided our own entertainment and took our bowling seriously.

The alley was halfway between Danville, where Geisinger was, and Bloomsburg. Across the highway was Brady's bar, where we watered after the games.

One night, I was on call for surgery, which should have prevented me from going. Skins phoned and asked my upper-level resident, Dr. Whiteman, "Do you like bowling?"

"Love it."

"The ER has a match tonight, but we're short one."

I saw the excitement in Dr. Whiteman's eyes. "I'm ready to go."

"No, not you. Joe Thek."

"I don't understand."

"Will you take his call, so he can bowl?"

There were priorities.

Priorities. I still thought death was the enemy, the number one priority. Early in my first year, we admitted a lady for an ascending paralysis due to Guillain-Barre syndrome. She lost control of her ability to breathe, and we put her on a respirator. I was on call every third night and saw her struggling.

During that fall and winter, we attempted to wean her from the blower but met with little success. We gave the woman a small blackboard to hold in her lap for communication. While attached to the respirator every morning, the lady wrote, "Let me die."

We couldn't let her die, so we carefully weaned her from the blower. At first, it was during the daytime for a few hours. Finally, the lady could go through the entire day without a respirator. On the first night after we completely weaned her, she passed on.

All that work, and she dies. All that work is down the drain.

Or was it? I learned that some things are worse than death and that not every death is premature. At least, I thought this. I realize now that it is never up to me or us, but HIM.

That first year, the ER bowling team placed second. It became my job to recruit residents who were good bowlers. When I interviewed students for the upcoming residency, one of my questions was, "What's your bowling average?"

Invariably, the interviewees thought I was kidding. They put in all that time, survived medical school, and now some jerk wanted to know their bowling averages.

However, I wasn't kidding.

If it's over 175, they're in automatically. If they can bowl that high, they must be able to stitch.

Isn't it good to know your doctor can roll a strike?

17

THE DIGBY FAMILY

On the day shift, I earned my initiation with twenty-four-year-old Elwood Digby. I went in to see him by myself. Perusing the chart, I walked into the room.

Hmm. No vital signs. Not very efficient.

"And what planet are you from?" a monotone voice asked as I entered.

I eyed a pathetic young man sitting on the gurney with a huge duffel bag overflowing with things. I surveyed his face. He had dilated pupils as if he were on cocaine. I got a sensation of looking into bottomless pits. On his feet were mismatched sneakers with one blue and one white sock. Two sweaters and a jacket covered his upper torso. Their sleeves hung down over his knuckles. On the back of his head was a worn CAT cap. But it was June.

I focused on a third sock that covered both ears and stretched across the hairline. Bobby pins anchored it to the scalp. A swimmer's nose plug in his nostrils completed the outfit.

"And what planet are you from?" he repeated.

"Earth." My voice quivered. *Oh great! A whacko.*

"Don't sound like you're too sure 'bout that."

"What seems to be the problem, eh, ... Elwood?" I retrieved the name on the chart and, while I did, composed myself. I had been taken off guard by this unusual person.

Whatever you think of him, remember you're a doctor. He came to you for help.

The patient didn't respond.

Does he hear me?

I reiterated the question, only louder.

"If I knew that, would I be here now?"

I scanned the chart again; no recorded blood pressure, pulse, or temperature. "My name is Doctor Thek, and I need to get your vital signs."

"Capricorn. Born on the cusp of the seventh moon."

"No, your vital signs!"

"Told you, Cap—"

"Blood pressure, pulse and—"

"Oh, them," Elwood winked. He dumped his duffel bag onto the sheet and sifted through old Kleenex, rubber bands, numerous combs, rosary beads, Tarot cards, batteries, K-Mart coupons, a light bulb, a TV remote control, a can of dog food, and a dozen other items.

"Let's see, my vital signs. Yes, I know they're here somewhere." Holding the light bulb over his head, Elwood exclaimed, "Good idea, huh?"

I gave up the idea of vital signs. Resigned that we couldn't get any, I reviewed the chart again. Elwood claimed to be allergic to psychedelic eggs, soap operas, and Pennsylvania.

This is nonsense! How can you be allergic to a whole state? Maybe he means penicillin.

I was starting to understand him, and that frightened me.

Once again, my focus became the sock on his head.

"Why are you wearing that 'ear sock?'"

"Nouns and verbs. Nouns and verbs," Elwood sing-songed.

Gritting my teeth in frustration, I eyed two wires ascending from the sweaters and ending on either side of his head beneath the sock. I heard something garbled emanating from the ears.

"Do you have a radio on?"

"Counter stimulus. Blocks out those unwanted voices. Gives any busy highway that library sound."

"Could you turn it off, so I can talk to you?"

He took off the camouflaged headphones and smiled.

"Why do you have the nose plug in?"

"Can't sneeze that way. Don't want me to lose my spirit, do you?"

I almost understood his response. Shivering, I paused a moment before asking, "Why did you come here?"

Elwood's attention wandered.

Finally, I repeated, "Why did you come?"

"The pulse."

I waited for an explanation, but none was forthcoming. "What pulse?"

"The Cosmic pulse, the endless drumbeat, the pacin' machine. Don't you know nothin'? What kind of a doctor are you anyway?"

"A good one, but I don't understand your complaint."

"The pump without water, the ticker without tape."

I studied the chart again. The nurse's note read, "Here to have pacemaker checked." I asked, "Do you have a pacemaker?"

With that, he removed the jacket, two sweaters, his flannel shirt, and a grimy undershirt. Petrified, I tried to fathom what he was doing, hoping he would show me his pacemaker scar.

Finally, he stood proudly before me, bare-chested. Tied around the neck with a boot lace was a transistor radio. "Wanna know if it's workin', Doc."

"If what's working?"

Elwood pointed to the radio. "My pacemaker. Is it givin' me the right beat?"

I didn't know what to say and stepped back.

##! Never covered this in Med School!

"Aren't you gonna check it, Doc? Can't you do an x-ray to see if it's working?"

I realized the only way out of the predicament was to go along with the patient's insanity. I reached behind his neck to untie the radio. He got into my crotch and pinched my gonads as I unknotted the string. I jumped backward and dropped the radio on the floor. It split in two, and one half slid across the floor toward the door, the other to the opposite wall.

Elwood put his hand to his throat and started to make a guttural, choking noise. His face turned deep purple.

Can the power of suggestion make a person choke to death like voodoo curses? Now is not the time to experiment.

I reached for the radio and stuck on some adhesive tape to hold the halves together.

Simultaneously, Dr. Ross appeared in the doorway. I gave him a look of embarrassment while Elwood continued to choke.

Without saying a word, Dr. Ross calmly took the radio and re-tied it around his neck.

"Your pacemaker's fine," Dr. Ross said. Then he left.

Elwood took his hand away from his throat and breathed normally. His color returned. I just stood there with my mouth open.

"Better close that before you catch some flies," Elwood said.

Now I'm getting advice from a nut!

I turned around toward the doorway.

"Say, ain't cha' gonna check my pacemaker?" he asked.

"Just did. It's fine." I said and left the room.

IT TURNED out that Dr. Ross had cured Elwood's father of impotence. Mr. Digby named his three sons after him.

"Curing him was my biggest mistake," Dr. Ross said.

One day, Mr. Digby and his other two sons appeared in the ER. The two boys beside him were like bookends. He was about five feet eleven, but they were big boys, about six feet five. The dad carried a jar filled with spiders. He plunked it on top of the counter.

"I want to know what kind of spiders these are."

I was sitting there reading. I lifted my head. "Are you talking to me?"

Mr. Digby nodded his head.

I looked at them. They were neither Brown Recluses nor Black Widows—the only two poisonous American spiders.

"I don't know what kind they are. Why do you want to know?"

"Because they're all over my house."

That doesn't surprise me.

"Don't worry, they're not poisonous," I said.

"How do you know if you don't know what kind they are?"

I was getting angry. Then, he lifted the jar off the counter, "Being this is the poison center, I know you have books, and you could look up the names of these spiders. Since you ain't, I'm gonna phone your boss and have you fired."

"Be my guest."

With that, the dad turned around and went through a doorway into the waiting room. The ER then sported windows between the nurses' station and the waiting room. The doctors could view the waiting room through them. If the nurses wanted to stop prying eyes from looking back, all they had to do was close the blinds.

Anyway, the sons followed him like puppies. I could see him through the windows. He placed a call. His face went from anger to happiness. Then, the dad hung up the phone and returned to the ER.

"Dr. Ross knew what kind of spiders these were!" Mr. Digby lifted the jar.

How did he know? Dr. Ross hasn't even seen them.

"What did he say?"

"Dr. Ross asked me one simple question. One, which you could've asked."

"What's that?"

"'Do they have wings?' I looked. I told him they didn't. He said, 'then, they must be land spiders.'"

With that, he held the jar aloft and ran out the door, yelling, "They're land spiders!"

ONE NEW YEAR'S EVE, a bad night for any ER, I was working. When we had a helicopter (more on that later), one resident was on call for it while the ER doc dispatched it. Anyway, I got a frantic call from a paramedic to dispatch the whirlybird because someone had fallen down the basement stairs. Now, he was paralyzed.

I thought I recognized the address. "The man who fell down the stairs, is that Elwood Digby?"

A flabbergasted paramedic answered, "Yes."

I ain't dispatching a helicopter for him.

"Then bring him in by ambulance," I said.

When they arrived, the paramedics put him on a gurney, and we put him into our big holding area where five drunks were already sleeping it off. I called it "veterinary medicine."

I pulled the curtains around him. I stuck needles in his feet, but he still didn't move.

Looks paralyzed. But I know Elwood. I don't know how he's doing it, but I'm sure he's faking it.

So, I started an IV, ran it wide open, and waited.

Pretty soon, Elwood arose to urinate. Upon returning, he was paralyzed again. I kept him with the five drunks overnight, and then he went home.

18

THE HELICOPTER

D r. Ross moved up in administration. Dr. Snow replaced him. In an ER meeting, the new director announced, "We need a helicopter."

"Are you joking?" I asked.

Dr. Snow didn't laugh. "The residents *will* fly."

That was it—no further discussion.

Plans for flying went ahead as if they had a life of their own. It was called "Life Flight." We required a new building with a landing pad and an elevator to take the patient directly to the units. So, we also moved out of the old ER and built a new one that could accommodate a helicopter. Everything was going up: the helicopter, the new ER, the census. Geisinger modernized and lost something in the transition. Before, it was more down to Earth – more intimate. It was now more modern, and we lost some patient contact in the change.

Then we had the residents' union meeting. There was a big brouhaha about flying.

At first, everybody wanted to go. The obstetrical residents thought they should be with the babies; the pediatric residents figured they should be with the kids, etc. The room was in an uproar.

"Wait a minute!" Paul Lewis, one of the ER residents a year behind me, stood and said.

We all turned to listen.

"What about insurance if the helicopter goes down?"

The room became quiet. Now, no one wanted to fly.

What happened the next day didn't help. There was an air crash involving a helicopter at a nearby hospital. All five people, including the patient, were killed. They should not have dispatched the chopper because of the weather. All the other residents refused to fly. Which meant the ER residents had to if a doctor was supposed to go on every flight as Geisinger had planned.

What are we doing, risking our lives? What about Edie and the kids?

But isn't that what you signed up for? A voice asked from deep inside me.

I guess so. Sometimes, to save lives, you have to risk yours. That's why doctors get the big bucks.

However, there is something almost romantic about a helicopter which makes residents want to fly, and paramedics enjoy dispatching it. But the chopper is a two-way flight. First, the patient waits for its arrival; then, they return to the hospital. If the accident trapped the patient in the vehicle, or if the patient has to travel over fifty miles, the helicopter makes sense because it's faster, and time is of the essence. However, if it's less than fifty miles and the patient can be moved, an ambulance is quicker to get them to definitive care. It's a one-way trip. They designed helicopters for rural areas like out in the West, not urban ones. You could crash into buildings here! And where do you land? The logistics can be a nightmare.

Try telling that to a Geisinger. The cost of having the whirlybird is enormous. There is the housing, the mechanic, the pilot, the flight nurses, the doctors, the special equipment, etc. The hospital has a vested interest in hoping all patients can be flown.

The cost was not the only problem we faced. The residency had to be increased to six people per year instead of the previous four to accommodate the helicopter program. We recruited Dominic (who had come to Geisinger as a resident in internal medicine and was a year behind me) and Sal Amani from within Geisinger. Sal was an orthopedic resident and was well-liked.

Flying became a required part of the residency. Because I was there before the chopper, it was my choice.

If I don't fly, many people will get mad at me.

So, I flew.

The flight crew followed the Susquehanna River, especially if it was foggy. We had to be alert for bridges. The helicopter traveled so low at times we almost stopped at red lights.

When I was in the air at night, I couldn't tell up from down. The stars were above, and below were the flickering lights of the countryside. They were sparse and looked like stars. The difference escaped me.

One day, I was on call when a boy severed his arm in a thresher. Our helicopter transported him to Johns Hopkins in Maryland, where they could do the microsurgery needed to re-attach his arm, which we put on ice. After dropping off him and his arm, the chopper re-fueled. My ears hurt badly. The helicopter doesn't have a pressurized cabin. After the trip, I took the easy way out and quit flying. By the end of the summer, the boy was throwing a baseball again.

19

LIFE OUTSIDE THE ER

E ven doctors are people. They need time off like everybody else.

When Edie and I went to Danville, Jimmy, our foster son, had stayed in Somerville. He was nineteen now. Jobs in New Jersey (including one where Jimmy dressed up as a bee) didn't pay enough, so he moved to Danville. He got a job as an orderly at Geisinger. Jimmy got his own place nearby.

After my first year of residency, Edie and I moved from Geisinger's property to a house around the corner from the hospital.

It had two stories with eight rooms but needed work. I painted the inside of the house with the help of a security guard named, Joe Simmond.

He gave us two giant wooden tables. We kept the orange one downstairs in the dining area where we ate. The brown table stayed upstairs, serving as an excellent desk. I started writing again, something I hadn't done since my days with the farm workers.

The previous owner had not weatherproofed the house. The present owner and I blew in insulation one weekend. When the furnace broke in winter, I took hot showers at the ER every day. We borrowed a kerosene heater that was supposed to run clean but didn't. It left a fine film on all our furniture.

Edie converted part of the backyard into a garden. When the grass left behind grew too long, the neighbor told me, "There might be snakes in there!"

"Snakes? Where?"

"You'd better cut it."

That was enough. The next day, I bought a lawn mower and cut the lawn. Who invented lawns anyway? However, I didn't find any snakes, but then again, they might have been hiding.

The house was suitable for our boys. There was a side porch and another in front with a fence along the street. The sidewalk was perfect for riding bicycles, and they took advantage of it.

DOMINIC CAME to Geisinger as a resident in Internal Medicine (a year behind me). He and I played poker at Dave Bain's (a resident in Pediatrics) house deep in the woods. It was a time to relax and escape from all the drama we saw daily

Brendon Nickel, another player, had some magic mushrooms. He threw them on the kitchen table and said, "Let's smoke these."

"What?" I replied. "Are you crazy? We'll get a fungus in our lungs! No, thanks! Beer is enough for me."

Brendon gave a mushroom to Jim Reims, another player and a resident in orthopedics. At four in the morning, Jim was out roaming in the woods and got lost. We were all drunk or stoned.

I don't know when public drunkenness became an ideal. It's an escape for anyone who believes that eat, drink, and be merry is all there is to life. You want to flee from the suffering, the death, the seeming meaninglessness of it all. Why not go out and party, for tomorrow, who knows what will happen?

If you have no hope, as we didn't, you take pleasure while you can and where you can. But that's a hollow philosophy, as I would find out.[1]

At the start of my second year, they placed me in the units with

John Starsky as my intern. He was a big guy, about 6'5" and 250, with unruly hair that made him look like Harpo Marx[2], who ate everything. I mean *everything*, even the crab shells that some dietician had stuffed. And fast! If you turned your head, he cleaned his plate. I swear Big John (as we called him) inhaled the food.

Before Big John, the on-call food was free. You could eat whatever was there. It was pretty good for hospital food. After Big John appeared, the hospital passed a measure stating the residents could only eat $9.00 worth of food while on call. I felt it was directed toward him and named it the "Starsky Rule."

Big John had suffered a nervous breakdown before coming to Geisinger. He was a patient in the psychiatric ward right before coming to the units for his first rotation as an intern. Can you imagine leaving the hospital and being stuck with me as an upper-level resident? Somebody wasn't thinking.

Big John lived in his car and flew an airplane. He lived in his car! I can't imagine getting on a plane and having him as a pilot. Despite that, he was all right. A little crazy, but hey, aren't we all? Big John fit right in, becoming one of the boys.

One night, we were playing cards at Dave Bain's house. Big John says, "I could really go for a Black Russian."

"A what?" I asked, unfamiliar with the term. I followed him into the kitchen with our host, Dave Bain.

"It's a drink. Give me some Vodka. Do we have any Kahlua?"

"What, do you think I'm a restaurant? No, I don't have any Kahlua," Dave said. "Will coffee do?"

"Sure."

Dave gave him a bottle of vodka and perked some coffee. When it was done, Big John poured more Vodka than coffee into a glass with ice and then took out his lighter.

"What are you gonna do with that?" I asked nervously.

"Watch."

His back to me, he lit the concoction. I was aghast, thinking that the glass would explode from the Vodka. Then Big John turned, and several strands of his hair had caught fire. We hurriedly put a moist towel on his head before he got burned.

At a picnic, we needed a cook for the grill. Big John volunteered. You could count him in if anything were remotely attached to food. The chef's hat appeared on his head. Then he ate raw hamburger paddies before they ever got to the grill. I stood there with my mouth agape. Yep, he was different, all right.

ANOTHER OF OUR favorite pastimes was bowling. In the ER, Paul Lewis was one of the new residents. I taught him how to hit a golf ball in the spring and played chess with him, too.

Paul could bowl. He taught me how to use a fingertip[3] ball. As previously said, I stacked the team. Since it was a handicapped league, it didn't pay to win by a lot. You wanted a small winning margin. Early in the season, we established low averages, also called sandbagging – or cheating. That's how I started whirl-a-bowl.

After we had already won., I whispered to Paul. "Watch this."

"What are you doing?"

I started toward the alley typically, spun around once, and then rolled. It made the person very dizzy. Think of holding up a sixteen-pound ball at arms-length and spinning simultaneously. You had to be an acrobat. The ball inevitably went in the gutter on the first roll. The next time the dizziness was not as bad. The ball stayed in the alley and knocked down a few pins.

Not to be outdone, Paul rolled lefty.

Afterward, all of us visited Brady's Bar. It was on the highway between Danville and the next town, Bloomsburg. In other words, it was a watering place in the middle of nowhere. I doubt they would've had any customers if it weren't for the bowling alley across the highway.

The building itself was unassuming. One you could easily miss it if you didn't know Brady's was there. And it was dark. Why is it that all bars are dark?

Anyway, Paul liked to buy the drinks and watch others make fools of themselves. Naturally, I drank.

"Bet you can't drink a whole bottle of Tequila," he said.

"You're on."

I looked at the bottom of the bottle, and there was something in there.

"What's that?" I asked, pointing to it.

"The worm. If you drink the whole thing, you get to eat it."

"Eat a worm? Don't think so."

"Okay. No worm"

I took a few gulps rapidly, then slowed down. The world tipped whenever I moved.

C'mon. Be a man. Just a few more gulps, an inner voice told me.

I slid off the chair and under the table. I took those gulps. But, more seemed to appear.

Where did that come from?

I took a few more swigs.

Almost there, the voice egged me on.

Finally, after about an hour, the bottle was empty!

"Done!" I slurred from beneath the table.

Paul had to drive me home.

∾

EDIE AND I took Dom and his wife, Aracely, bowling. Dom retrieved his ball at the return, swiveled, and rolled.

"Dom, get closer to the foul line and bowl off your left leg," I advised.

Dom still fired from the return.

"Closer to the foul line!"

Dom rolled from the ball return again. The ball went into the gutter. That wasn't bad enough. It was in the wrong alley! The bowler in the next lane wasn't happy. I never took Dom to the alley again.

∾

ANOTHER RECRUIT WAS TIM BERNARD. He had a chicken that laid green eggs.

"Those would be good for St. Patrick's Day," I told him. Funny the things we remember.

When Tim went to Dartmouth, his wife stayed in California. She didn't like him improving himself and desired a grease monkey. We all have to make sacrifices to get where and what we want.

20

THE SECOND YEAR AT GEISINGER

In 1980, Edie became pregnant again. We called her "Fertile Myrtle."

Anyway, around Thanksgiving, she went into labor.

"We have to start an IV," the nurse informed us.

"Don't touch me!" Edie insisted. "Get my husband. He can start it."

"Whatever you say, princess," the nurse replied facetiously.

"Get some warm, wet compresses for the arm," I ordered, knowing from experience that Edie was not an easy stick.

I poked her after waiting for her veins to pop out from the heat. Finally, we had an IV after several blown attempts.

After a few hours of no activity, the nurse came in and says, "Bad news. She's in false labor. Looks like we have to take your IV out so you can go home." She moved toward the bed.

"Wait a *#*# minute!" Edie shouted. "I'm not going through this again! Isn't there some way we can save the IV?"

The nurse stopped and scratched her chin. "Well, we could cap it if someone was willing to flush it with heparin[1]."

They both looked at me. What could I say? "Of course, I'll do it!"

So, I had not only started Edie's IV, but now I was responsible for its maintenance. I took her home and flushed the heparin lock a few times daily.

A few days later, Edie went into actual labor.

"Keep away from me, you #*#*!" she screamed when I tried to comfort her.

On November 30, 1980, our daughter, Shannon, was born. We finally had a girl! She immediately stole my heart.

Right after delivery, Edie had her tubes tied. We figured four kids was enough. She wanted me to get a vasectomy to make sure. I nearly did, but GOD gave me a haunting dream about my Aunt Angie.

What about Little Eddie? What if I want another child?

I couldn't do it.

Edie and I agonized about Shannon's name. If she were a boy, we chose the name 'Jordan.' He could join the 'J' club, and it was Jewish. Edie and I figured if we could name a boy after a river, why not a girl? We considered 'Merced,' the river's name at the base of Half Dome. But, neither of us is Hispanic. I read how the Shannon River started when a teenage girl was told by her parents to stay away from a particular well. She went anyway, fell in, and died. The well gushed forth a river of water named "Shannon." We decided that was a good name. Her middle name is Kelly.

Mom would like that.

AFTER I'D SURVIVED the first year, I became part of the club. Some didn't and needed replacement—interns like the ER's own Bob Bagley. However, things were changing. As upper-level residents, we were supposed to act superior to the "lowly" interns. However, for a variety of reasons, we didn't. Having gone through the initiation process recently, we were more sympathetic toward the interns, not arrogant.

DURING MY SECOND YEAR, I directed interns to do the work, hopefully with compassion. We supervised students, too. We had a motto for any procedure, "Watch one, do one, teach one." That was how you gained "experience."

Anyway, that's how I met Tom Major. He was two years behind me, a student from Dominic's osteopathic school. Tom came over to my house during lunch many times. Both of us played guitars and sang songs we wrote.

The ER docs took melodies from the radio and gave them new words. Like *Open Arms* by Journey[2]. "So now I come to you with open arms ... " we changed to "So now I come to you with broken arms ... " Or Harry Belafonte[3]'s *Banana Boat Song (Day-O,)* we changed to *Bell-y Pain.* I still remember some of the words.

IF YOU'RE FEELIN' sick
 And you're throwin' up all over,
 Belly pain come to the ER. (in the background)
 You'd better come quick
 Or you'll be pushin' up the clover.

BELL-Y! Bell-y pain! Belly pain come to the ER.
 Bell-y! Bell-y Pain! Bell-y pain come to the ER.

THEN YOU START to shiver
 And your heart goes pitter-patter.
 Belly pain come to the ER. (in the background)
 It could be your liver,
 Pancreas or bladder!

BELL-Y! Bell-y pain! Belly pain come to the ER.
 Bell-y! Bell-y Pain! Bell-y pain come to the ER.

. . .

WE DRESSED in straw hats to sing the song. Some people would be offended by the jingle, but we meant it to be delivered tongue-in-cheek. We had other songs, and there were other parties where you could bet we made fools of ourselves. I developed a knack for changing lyrics.

Love me, Love me, Love me, I'm an administrator, I wrote to the tune of Phil Ochs *Love me, Love Me, Love Me, I'm a Liberal.* Somehow, the words got posted on the bulletin board. I thought I would get fired, but the big-wigs never discovered I was the author.

One of my second-year rotations was in psychiatry. I went to the prison to interview two women who were purportedly on a fast.

The female guard took me aside. "I think they're faking it. Probably getting candy from the other prisoners. We need you to say they're crazy so we can give them water intravenously."

I saw the two women.

"Why are you here?" I asked of two emaciated women, one white and one black with dreadlocks.

No answer.

Thinking they may not have heard, I very deliberately said, " W-h-y A-r-e Y-o-u H-e-r-e?"

Again, no answer.

"The sky is green today."

No answer.

I closed my notebook, saying, "I'm wasting my time," and left the cell.

Outside, I asked the guard, "What are they in for?"

She informed me, "They're whores of John Africa.[4] They took over a building in Philadelphia. There was a shootout. Finally, they gave themselves up. The girls refused to test for syphilis and TB once in prison. Hence, the so-called fast."

"They're not crazy, sociopathic maybe, but not nuts."

"You mean we can't stick an IV in 'em?"

"No, you can't."

The guard was angry because I denied her the IVs. Honestly, I didn't know who was crazier, the inmates or the guards.

THERE WAS ALSO A NIGHT SHIFT. It was natural for me—quiet and laid back. Only the really sick or the really crazy came in. You could pull practical jokes, and no one seemed to care.

One of the night shift nurses was Linda Lutz. Every night, Linda visited the bathroom at least once before going home. We also had a large skeleton on wheels for instruction.

It'll scare the crap out of her.

One night, I switched off the light in the bathroom. I made eyes out of little paper cups and put them on the skeleton. Then, I put a cigarette in its mouth. I wheeled the six-foot body of bones into the unlit bathroom and waited for Linda to go. At about six, I heard her scream.

I STARTED IVs BECAUSE, as I said, there was no IV team. When I was on call, they beeped me on the pager if an IV had infiltrated. I became good at starting them. You had to be to eat. We would be in the residents' room, watching TV or playing ping-pong, pool, or backgammon. Then, the pager would go off. One night, one of the residents was about to win a game of ping-pong when his pager sounded. He got so angry that he flushed his pager down the toilet. As he did, the pager went off, "Dr. Wright, report to the ER. Report to the ER."

On another night on-call, the Miracle of Lake Placid occurred. We saw most of the hockey game on the TV in the residents' lounge. When the U.S. beat the Russians for the gold medal, it was like the '69 Mets all over again. Nobody expected it—an amateur team won against the pros. An analogy would be Notre Dame beating the Super Bowl champ.

WE WORKED HARD and long hours in the units. Having Big John there made it easier. However, because I had more "experience," I became primarily responsible for a young woman in her thirties. She had been transferred from another hospital. The doctors there did their modern imitation of Pontius Pilate by washing their hands of her.

Oh, great! How'm I gonna figure her out?

We had no idea what was wrong with her, but she was unconscious, on a respirator, and her blood pressure was dangerously low (about 40). Everything shut down: her kidneys, her liver, her lungs. In other words, Anna was a train wreck.

However, she had a rash. It was a clue. Like Sherlock Holmes, I took out a magnifying glass and examined it.

Hmm. All over her body.

Then, Dr. Ayab, another resident, brought in an article about a new disease, Toxic Shock Syndrome (TSS). "This might be interesting," he said and left it for me. I started to read it. The article really caught my attention with the words, "… accompanied by a whole-body rash …" Those words fairly jumped off the page.

I read on.

That's Anna, alright. The symptoms fit her to a "T."

It turned out that she had her period and was using tampons. Now, we had a diagnosis and had jumped the first hurdle.

Toxic Shock Syndrome. Never heard of it. But I'm sure syphilis was new once, too.

Anna's hands peeled and her eyes suffered conjunctivitis. I learned then that the skin is an organ too. We often forget that and neglect our skin. Amid all the machines, it wasn't easy to care for her.

I was determined that she was not going to die on my shift. Every night I watched the monitors as Anna slowly improved. Finally, she was able to go to her home. Because both of us were non-believers then, Anna and I thought it was my work. Actually, SOMEONE else was taking care of her all the time.

There is an adage in research medicine: "Publish or perish." So, the attending and I wrote and published about my experience with Anna and TSS.

21

THE RESIDENTS' UNION

A residents' union encompassed about one hundred and fifty doctors in most disciplines at Geisinger Hospital. A doctors' union? Yes! I attended the meetings every month. It was responsible for the moonlighting schedule. The residents did a lot of extra time because they weren't paid much. With my background, I was a natural.

For the first two years, I didn't miss a meeting. However, then the president graduated, and the residents needed a replacement. They voted. Unfortunately for me, I couldn't attend. I missed my first meeting and the vote. While I was absent, they elected me president with Dominic as vice president.

That'll teach me not to miss a meeting.

Dominic was in charge of moonlighting and was called "The Don." He decided who went where and when.

Moonlighting was especially hard driving through snow and ice. We all were tired, so we wanted twenty-four-hour shifts to make it worth our while. How would you like to be in the hands of a resident in his twenty-third hour of sleeplessness?

Once, I was in St. Joe's ER in Hazelton atop a mountain, the highest city in Pennsylvania. It snowed all day, some nine inches.

No one's gonna drive up here in this. I'm stuck.

I was amazed when fellow resident Phil Bocco came into the ER during the shift change. He not only made it. Phil was on time!

"Am I glad to see you!" I exclaimed

Phil just shrugged as if it was nothing. I never forgot it.

As the president, I became responsible for the residents' salaries, who flew in the helicopter, and for taking care of the nuns at St. Cyril's, a nearby Czech nunnery.

I was surprised when I was invited to a medical staff meeting to represent the residents discussing everyone's salaries.

I can see Dr. Ross' fingerprints in this.

Attending physicians from every discipline were there and held it in a regular classroom. There were the everyday pre-meeting conversations. As president of the hospital, Doctor Ross sat behind a desk, a gavel in his hand, presiding over the meeting. Beside him stood the bulky Dr. Humphrey, who was the sergeant-of-arms.

Wonder how he got that job. Was it his size? He's almost as big as Big John.

"Order! Order!" Dr. Ross shouted in his distinctive high-pitched voice while banging the gavel on the desk. I think he enjoyed doing that. Everyone immediately took their seats. "I've called you tonight to discuss my favorite subject–money," he continued dryly, trying to keep a straight face. "It's a little tight this year."

Dr. Mancuso from cardiology stood up and said, "I suggest we keep the resident's salary the same."

I saw red. We worked about eighty hours a week for $14,000 a year, which meant we were *already* under the minimum wage[1].

I could take a lot, but Dr. Mancuso had pushed the wrong button. Back then, I spouted off when angry, like the end of a water hose. It didn't happen often, but I became totally uncaring about the fallout when it did.

I stood up immediately, "We are not your slaves! We do all the scut work[2] so you can play golf! It's outrageous! If we don't get a raise, we'll –we'll strike!"

You would've thought I dropped a bomb in the room. A hush came over everyone as the doctors glared at me. I began to say something, but Skins, there representing the ER, pulled on my proverbial white coat.

"Sit down," he whispered. "You've made your point. Don't mess it up."

I was ushered into the hall by Dr. Humphrey. The door was closed behind me as they voted on the proposal.

Oh great! We do all the work and don't get to vote!

I was still fuming. After a little while, I calmed down and felt remorseful.

What have I done? I can have a big mouth. Maybe I should apologize.

I waited impatiently in the hallway for a few minutes. In the interim, I cooled off.

Finally, the door opened, and the sergeant-of-arms motioned to me with his finger to re-enter. As I did, Skins caught my gaze. He put his finger to his lips. I kept quiet (which was very, very hard)[3].

"Shh!" he whispered when I sat next to him. "You've won."

The resident's salary went from $14,000 a year to $18,000. Dr. Ross had convinced the attending physicians to take a pay cut to supply the money.

"We don't want to have trouble with our residents," Skins told me later that he had said.

Overnight, I'd become a hero to some. I thought it was all my doing. It's good that we have gravity, or I'd be floating in space somewhere because so much hot air filled me. However, there was SOMEONE behind the scenes, a Sovereign GOD. Yes, I have free will and can choose to disobey HIM, like taking my father's car down the shore. How HE works it out, I don't know. I'm not GOD. I'm just glad that HE does.

THERE WERE STILL THE POOR, old nuns. They paid far less than what a resident earned moonlighting in an ER, five dollars an hour compared to twenty-five or thirty. Nobody wanted to care for them. I tried to convince Family Practice that it would be a good experience, but they weren't interested. So, the responsibility fell on me. There I was, this agnostic doctor, taking care of Czech nuns. At first, I didn't like the nurse, Sister Leona. Her broad shoulders and short legs looked like a fullback for the Green Bay Packers.

Maybe I should call her Jim Taylor[4].

However, GOD doesn't look at a person's exterior but at their heart[5].

One early morning, around 4 a.m., the phone rang.

Who could this be? Maybe Johnny from Japan.

"Hello?" I answered sleepily.

"I'm sorry to wake you so early, but Sister Charles Mary has belly pain and needs to be seen," a calm Sister Leona said into the receiver.

"Can't it wait until a more reasonable hour?"

"I don't think so.

She, don't think so! Who's the doctor here? But there'll be no peace until I go.

"I'll be right over," I replied curtly.

En route, I realized what was ahead.

Should do a pelvic exam for any woman's belly pain. But she's a nun! Especially her. Probably hasn't had a pelvic in years. Maybe never!

When I walked through the doorway, Sister Leona already had Sister Charles up in stirrups with a white sheet draped across her belly and legs. Sister Charles, an elderly nun, maybe 90, moaned in obvious pain on the examining table.

"Gloves, please," I said.

Sister Leona immediately gave me a pair of plastic, Latex gloves.

What will I find?

I inserted my right hand into her birth canal. I felt a big mass toward the front.

Can't miss that tumor. Must be uterine or ovarian cancer.

I withdrew my hand. Sister Leona had a telephone in hers.

"What's that for?" I asked.

"For the ambulance."

"Oh, yeah. Call one. She has to go to the hospital."

Sister Leona dialed. In ten minutes, the paramedics lifted her gingerly off the examining table, and we went to the hospital five minutes away. Sister Charles moaned in pain all the way

Once in the ER, I felt a tugging on my sleeve. It was Sister Leona.

"Now what?" I asked.

In her perfect English, she asked, "Aren't you going to put a Foley[6] in?"

"Give me a minute."

"No, now."

"Oh, okay. If it will make *you* feel better," I replied sarcastically. "Ma Williams[7], put a catheter in."

When she did, we got about a liter and a half of urine in the bag. Sister Charles stopped writhing in pain. Instantaneously, she became more comfortable.

I did another pelvic. The mass was gone.

I looked at Sister Leona, who was trying to stifle a smile.

"Why, you sly dog! You knew all along, didn't you?"

She nodded.

"Then why didn't you tell me?" I asked.

"I'm just a nurse. You're the doctor. Would you have listened?"

"Ouch!"

"As it was, we did everything in good time."

We had a good laugh. I learned to always listen to the nurses, especially Sister Leona.

She never awakened me again. When a nun passed on in the night, Sister Leona even waited until the morning before calling me to sign a death certificate.

"Didn't want to bother you," she'd say in her humble way.

"Thanks."

On holidays, the room was full of flowers. For Christmas, it was poinsettias. My nose ran all day. It was like working at a florist. But they loved me and were very appreciative.

Thought I was doing them a favor. Looks like they did one for me.

22

BILL

There wasn't any penetrating trauma[1] in Danville. So, I went to Pittsburgh and the Center for Emergency Medicine. I met Bill Ranetsky, a supervisor of paramedics, there. He was a couple of years older than I, with dark, moon-swept hair.

On his desk, there was a chessboard with pieces. He noticed me eyeing them.

"Wanna play?" he asked.

I nodded.

He removed a rook's pawn from his side to give me an advantage.

Then, he started to talk. "Hear you know something about Toxic Shock Syndrome."

Now how in the world would he know that? Must've read my article. I thought as we made several moves.

"And helicopters, too."

Why is he buttering me up?

We made several more moves. Before I knew it, I was hopelessly lost.

Triumphantly, he said, "Checkmate," as if he'd won a Wimbledon match.

"Another game?" I asked.

"Not now. Too busy."

I suspect he wanted to savor the moment. After all, a paramedic had beaten a doctor.

We became good friends and did many things together. He even introduced me to his parents and boys.

Bill had been married twice before and divorced both times. He hadn't met Mary yet, who would become his third and final wife. The second marriage didn't last long, and Bill didn't consider it a marriage. He had two sons from his first marriage, Jason and David. They were about Josh and Jeremiah's ages. His parents raised them, and they lived in nearby East McKeesport.

We went there often to see them and his boys. It was an unusual situation.

Bill liked to play video games in an arcade. There was one called *Asteroid* that we often stopped to play with just before getting to his parent's house. Their house was full between them, the two boys, and the father's brain-challenged brother.

On the way there one night, we stopped at a pizzeria. I looked at the menu. "Do you have any mussels?" I asked the waitress.

She flexed her elbow.

Bill laughed. "Guess not," he said. "Just give us a regular pizza."

After she had left, I asked, "What happened with your first wife?"

"Do you like anchovies?" he asked, looking at a menu.

Maybe he didn't hear me. "What happened with your first wife?" I repeated in a stronger voice.

"What about mushrooms?"

He doesn't want to talk about it. Have to let it go.

"They're both okay," I answered. "My nephew calls anchovies 'mustaches.'"

Bill laughed, then said, "Next time, we'll order both."

One evening, we were on our way to a Las Vegas Night hosted by the police. All the games involved gambling and were illegal. That's a hoot! However, who's going to arrest the police? They had confiscated all the games in raids. The proceeds would go to the PBA.

We were on our way there, in the slow lane of a four-lane highway with two lanes in each direction. There was no divider. We were doing about forty when all we saw were red brake lights ahead of us. Bill jammed on his brake and stopped just before crashing into the car in front of him. I nearly hit the dashboard. Cars in the other direction stopped for no apparent reason.

"What is it now?" Bill asked.

We soon found out. A pedestrian was weaving in and out of traffic, obviously in a daze.

Is he drunk?

He stopped beside our car on the shoulder. Suddenly, he began to seize. Immediately, Bill and I left the car to tend to the man before he fell and hit his head on the asphalt. What are the odds of an ER doctor and a paramedic being in the vehicle you approach?

We coaxed him onto the grass on the other side of the berm before he could injure himself.

A cop pulled up.

"Get out of the way!" he barked. "You're holding up traffic!"

"But I'm a doctor, and he's a paramedic. This man has had a seizure and needs help."

"Get out of the way," he repeated, "or I'll arrest you both!"

I shrugged my shoulders, and we got in Bill's car, leaving the man on the side of the road. We proceeded to the Lost Wages, I mean Las Vegas, night. We entered a dimly lit building. The cops had put up Roulette wheels, dice tables, and card tables. Cops guarded a couple of kegs of beer near the front.

"Guess they're not worried about drinking and driving," I said, nodding toward the kegs.

"Not tonight."

We played cards until the wee hours of the morning, sipping our beers.

I STAYED at the University of Pittsburgh dormitory. Every night, I listened to Kool and the Gang[2]'s *Celebrate* overhead. For some reason, picketers were screaming something outside the dormitory.

A few years ago, that would've been me.

I just wanted to sleep. Pulling the pillow over my head, I blocked the sounds and dozed off.

The next day I went to Mercy Hospital, followed by Presbyterian Hospital in two weeks. Penetrating trauma–gun and stab wounds–came through their ERs.

Presby, and Allegheny (a third hospital) were at war over a helicopter. It landed at the Pitt football field to get a helicopter into the city, so both hospitals wanted to build a heliport. Allegheny eventually got a chopper. When Presby acquired theirs, Allegheny got a second. I didn't want to get involved, especially after a helicopter crashed into the river.

Bill wanted me to teach a dog lab[3] at the Center.

"This is how you intubate," I showed the paramedics. "To start a central line, you do this," and I poked the dog with a needle and catheter. I recalled the adage, "Watch one, do one, teach one."

Bill's family was very unusual. The Communist Party threw his grandfather out of the Party for being too radical. Bill was, unfortunately, raised an atheist. He looked at it as fortunate.

Ronald Reagan, our new president, gave a speech on television. I didn't care for him as Governor of California, and I certainly didn't like him as president. What was I thinking? That's okay; he probably wouldn't have cared for me either.

I went on ambulance runs and met other paramedics. They invited me to a bar where Bill played chess with the Pennsylvania state champ, who was also a policeman.

I sat down with a beer to watch the game. Bill made an awful move.

"What are you doing?" I whispered.

"Hustling. There's a mark I've been working on all night. After this game is over, he'll challenge me to one."

The State Champ finished him off in a couple of moves. Fulfilling Bill's prediction, a half-drunk young man sauntered to the table dressed in a cowboy hat, denim shirt with sequins, dungarees, and boots. He slammed a twenty-dollar bill on it.

"Partner, that twenty is for the winner."

"No, I can't take your money," Bill objected.

The man took out another twenty and slammed it down.

"Who says you're gonna win?"

"If you insist."

"I do."

After a few moves, Bill had him hopelessly bamboozled. Finally, Bill moved, gave me a wink, and said, "Checkmate."

The young man reached for the knife on his belt. The State Champ showed his belt with a gun attached and said, "I wouldn't do that if I were you."

Bill picked up the two twenties and left.

23

PRACTICAL JOKES

After the rotation in Pittsburgh, I returned to Geisinger and Edie. We were accustomed to taking separate vacations, so my absence was not a hardship for either of us. That was my rationalization.

We were constantly pulling practical jokes on each other. Some may seem crude or unfeeling now, but please remember what we did. Every day, we faced death and dying. Humor was an excellent way to vent. We always had an unwritten rule in joking—no one was to get hurt.

Dominic served his second year with Sal Amani in Emergency Medicine. The set-up was perfect for me.

Time to have a little fun.

On March 15th, I called Dom. Ara, his wife, answered.

"Hello?" she answered with a thick Spanish accent.

I stated, "Beware the Ides of March."

She immediately hung up. I didn't know they were having trouble with a peeping Tom. Ara had become anxious when she thought he had called.

Not learning my lesson, I called again on Tax Day, April 15th.

"Is Doctor Ruffalo there?" I asked gruffly.

The babysitter answered, "Doctor and Mrs. Ruffalo are out to dinner."

"This is Mr. Hochstetter with the IRS," I pretended. "Doctor Ruffalo is in a lot of trouble for cheating on his income taxes. He'd better call me back."

And I left my number, figuring Dominic would return the call and we'd have a good laugh.

I didn't know that the babysitter's father was the accountant who did Dominic's taxes. She went home and reportedly cried, "Daddy, the IRS is after Doctor Ruffalo!"

When Dom came to work the next day, he looked worried, saying, "The IRS is after me."

I kept quiet. I think Dom is still waiting for them to audit him.

ON A HELICOPTER FLIGHT, Doctor Tim Barnard did an outstanding job. The patient went to Williamsport Hospital, where a neurosurgeon operated on him. Dom called Tim and pretended to be that brain surgeon. "You did vel-ly, vel-ly bad job," he said, summoning up an Oriental accent.

"What!" Tim exploded. He ran into Dr. Ross in the hall, who happened to be passing through the ER.

"I just got off the phone with this neurosurgeon in Williamsport," Tim began. You could see the red face and hear the pressure of speech. "This guy is a real nut! He said I did a very bad job!" And Tim was off. He gave Dr. Ross an earful.

Dom and I approached them, and Dom tugged on Tim's sleeve.

"Not now. I'm busy!" he said with some annoyance. "Now, where was I? This hick surgeon—"

Again, Dom tugged on Tim's sleeve. He pulled his arm away and said, "Get away, will you? Can't you see I'm talking?"

"But it was me," Dom whispered, so only Tim and I heard.

He didn't understand and continued to criticize the neurosurgeon. "He's a real jerk. If I could get my hands—" he stopped in mid-sentence.

Suddenly, the idea popped into his head that it wasn't the brain surgeon calling but Dominic. Who knows what Dr. Ross thought? Maybe that Tim was maturing before his eyes and had the confidence to take jibes thrown at him. I wish that were true of all of us, and we could listen to JESUS and turn the other cheek.

～

THE NEXT DAY, I had planned to make my weekly visit to the nuns. I got in my car on the street and put the key in the ignition.

Grrr! Grrr! The engine murmured. I tried again. Grrr! Grr!

It sounded like it wanted to crank but wouldn't turn over.

Must be the starter. Have to call the nuns.

I went inside and called the nunnery.

"Hello. Sister Leona."

"This is Doctor Thek. My car won't start. Might have to cancel my visit this week."

"Why? Call a taxi. We'll pay."

"Good idea! Thanks."

And that's what I did, but I couldn't help wondering, *Did someone put something in the gas tank? Hope it's not an egg.*

We towed the car to my mechanic.

"When will it be ready? I asked.

"Tomorrow," he assured me in his bib overalls. The mechanic had oil smeared on his face, and I saw him only occasionally because he usually buried his head under the hood of a car. I became very familiar with the back of his head and the grime beneath his fingernails.

I left the garage on foot. Being without wheels was not a hardship since I walked to the ER. I wouldn't need it until next week to see the nuns.

Don't use the car a lot anyway.

～

I WAS on one night in the ER, and Dominic was doing his psychiatry rotation. I got a frantic call from a paramedic on the radio.

"This is Doctor Thek, at Geisinger—Over."

"You're not gonna believe this—Over."

What is it now?

"What you got?—Over."

"A naked lady is running down the street screaming in Spanish. And she's a karate expert—Over."

"A karate expert? How do you know that—Over."

"Her husband told us—Over."

"Bring him in, too—Over."

When they arrived, we placed the patient in the psych room. She took a seat in the corner away from us. She was naked, all right. The blanket on her didn't conceal everything. I went into the hallway while the nurse stayed with the patient and got her something to wear. The husband arrived. He was an older man, maybe fifty-five or sixty, with gray hair.

Something is wrong here.

"Please stick around and interpret for us," I said.

"Can't. Don't speak Spanish."

"Excuse me. Aren't you married?"

"Unfortunately."

"Well, then, how do you communicate?"

"With our hands."

"Sign language?"

He laughed. "No. Pointing. If I want her to get something, I point."

"What about her?"

"I don't understand."

"Does she point, too?"

Again, he laughed. "I think I should explain a few things. Let's go to another room. Someplace more private."

It had been a slow night until then, and there were no other patients in the ER. I invited the husband into one of the examining rooms and shut the door behind us. I directed him to sit on the gurney and pulled up a chair.

"I'm all ears," I said. "Shoot!"

"Remember when Carter was president, he gave asylum to about 125,000 people[1] that had come from Cuba?"

I remembered vaguely. So, I nodded.

"Many wanted to stay permanently in the US, like Maria, my wife. But to stay here, she had to be married."

"And you accommodated?"

"That's right."

Cuba? Dom's wife, Aracely, is from there. He speaks Spanish. He's also on psych. Maybe he can help?

"Ma Williams!" I shouted. "Can you get me, Dr. Ruffalo, on the phone!"

A groggy Dom answered me.

"What's up?" he asked.

"I have a lady, thirty-five or so, who was found naked in the middle of her street. To make matters worse, she speaks only Spanish. That's where you come in. I need you to interpret."

"Where's she from?"

"Cuba."

"I'll be right in."

"One other thing," I said in a hushed tone.

"What's that?"

"Stay away from her feet."

"Why do they stink?"

"No, she's a karate expert."

"You're kidding, right?"

"No. I wish I was. This is for real."

When Dominic arrived, he took the seat farthest away from her and closed the door to interview her. He must've been shaking in his boots. I heard voices coming from the room, mostly hers. After about a half-hour, the door opens, and Dominic comes out.

We sat in a private room.

"Well, what did you find?" I asked.

"She's not crazy."

"What? Normal people don't appear nude in the middle of their street, screaming at three in the morning!"

"Under normal circumstances, I'd agree with you."

"What do you mean?"

"Given the opportunity, she ran. She's been his sex slave since they got married. He's the one that should be locked up." Then he explained the situation. She was always to be at his beck and call, to do whatever he wanted.

I let that percolate. Then I asked, "What are we gonna do with her? We can't let her go back to that slime-ball."

"We'll admit her for at least three days. That should give social services enough time to investigate the home."

And that's the last I heard about it. Working in the ER was like taking a snapshot. If you wanted the whole movie, you needed more time. Speaking of more time, that's what my mechanic kept saying about my car.

"Is my car ready?" I asked my mechanic over the phone.

"I think I found the reason it won't start. A potato was in your exhaust."

"A potato in the exhaust? How does that stop the car from starting?'

"Simple. The potato keeps the engine from getting rid of fumes. It can't take in new air, either If no air comes in, it can't mix with the fuel —thus, there is no fire explosion to move the cylinder and crankshaft. The engine, without air coming in to mix with fuel, can't fire. So, the car won't start. The real question is, how did the potato get there, to begin with?"

I know. Dominic, watch out.

ON ANOTHER NIGHT, we had a psych patient named John. He was a lost soul with a belly that overhung his pants and different colored shoelaces. I don't know why my eyes kept going back to those shoelaces. I wanted to ask him why.

His answer will probably not make sense.

I tried to avert my eyes, but, like a magnet, they returned to those shoelaces. When I couldn't stand it any longer, I finally blurted out, "Why two different colored shoelaces?"

There was silence for a little while. I expected some profound answer.

Did he hear me?

I repeated the question.

"Oh, that," he finally said. "I lost one. This one fits, so, I wear it."

"Why not wear the other one, too, instead of the one that doesn't match?"

"What do you have OCD[2] or something? Who cares?"

This is a case for psych.

I called Dominic in to see him.

After Dom had interviewed John, Dom took me aside and said, "I think he's okay to be released. Just needs his meds adjusted."

The next evening, after I had taken my nap, I thought I'd pull a practical joke on Dominic and get him back for the car. I walked back to the ER and dialed his number.

An unsuspecting Dominic answered. "Hello?"

"This is Joe. You shouldn't have discharged that psych patient from the ER last night."

"Why not?" he asked nervously.

"Because he went berserk at the mall and shot a couple nuns."

"What? How hurt were they?"

"Dunno. They're in surgery now."

"I'll be right in."

I alerted the unit desk clerk, who agreed to go along with the joke.

He'll believe it if he sees me with a nun. Now, where can I get a nun? I know, Sister Leona!

I called the dispensary at the nunnery.

"Hello, Sister Leona."

"Hello, this is Doctor Thek. I need a favor."

I could almost see her straighten up. "What is it?"

I explained the situation to her.

"You mean you want me to deceive him?" she asked. "That would be like lying. I can't do it."

The line went dead for a few moments, then Sister Leona said, "What if I was going to the ER for another reason?"

"Like?"

"Like picking you up. You said your car was in the shop this week."

"That's right. It won't start."

"Sister Robert needs someone to look at her ear. What say I pick you up in fifteen minutes? If your friend sees us, I'm not responsible for his thoughts."

"Perfect! I'll be ready in fifteen. Do I need an otoscope[3]?"

"No. We have one here."

Dominic arrived to see me and Sister Leona in the ER waiting room. He took one look at her habit and disappeared. Who knows what he thought? I went with Sister Leona to examine Sister Robert's ear. She had an ear infection and I prescribed some antibiotics. Sister Leona dropped me at home on her way to the pharmacy.

The next day, I picked up my car. It turned over without a problem.

24

SOCCER COACH

An old proverb goes something like this: "If you want something done, ask a busy person." Indeed, that was true in my case.

The boys were young. I was more than just a resident, being their father, too. There should be classes in high school on how to be a parent. Sadly, we concentrate on silly things that we will hardly ever use. We should pay more attention to the most challenging job in the world – being a good parent. There are too many who don't take it seriously.

When Jeremiah was around five, Edie wanted him to join the local soccer team.

"It'll be good for him. Give him more confidence in himself," she said.

"I agree."

There was one little problem, though. No one wanted to be the assistant coach. The head coach, Coach Moore, called a meeting at a nearby conference hall, and he presided.

"Order! Order!" Coach Moore shouted into the raucous din engulfing us, slamming the gavel he had on a table in front of him. "Everyone, take your seats!"

We did, and all the parents in the big hall became silent.

"Everybody knows why we're here," Coach Moore said with his granite-like jaw. "We need an assistant coach. Any volunteers?"

Nobody did.

"We need someone to take care of cuts and bruises."

All eyes shifted to me.

"Whoa! I don't know anything about soccer," I said defensively.

"That don't matter," Coach Moore said. "Having an assistant who doesn't know soccer is good."

"A soccer coach who doesn't know soccer? How is that a 'good thing?'"

"Because you can leave the coaching to me and won't interfere. Besides, all I really need is someone to keep them away from the river."

"The river?" I asked.

"Yep. The place where they play is next to a stream. Keeping the kids away during practice and coaching is hard for me. When they do play, they kick each other in the shins. They get bruised mostly. Sometimes cut."

"Sounds like you need a nurse."

"Or a doctor."

Again, all eyes riveted on me. What could I do?

"Okay. I'll do it," I mumbled reluctantly.

I have to admit it was fun. I don't know who learned more about soccer—the kids or me. They made me laugh, and there is not enough laughter in this world. After grueling shifts in the ER, they always gave me a new perspective on life.

Jeremiah's team played on an American football field with a stream beside it. It wasn't deep—maybe one or two feet at its deepest spot. At its shallow points, you could walk across and barely get wet. There were many stones on the shore. However, it was like a magnet for the kids. I had to be ever vigilant.

One practice, I looked around, and there was no Jeremiah!

I ran down the embankment and spotted him by the stream.

"What *are* you doing?" I screamed at him as he picked up a stone and threw it in the water.

"Skimming stones!" he replied.

"Get back on the field! You scared me to death!"

He threw one last stone. It made several skips across the gurgling water before sinking.

"Not flat enough," Jeremiah mumbled.

"Go!"

He ran up the stream's bank and back to the football field.

"Play your positions!" Coach Moore was repeatedly yelling. It seemed like a lost cause. When someone kicked the ball, everyone ran to it–the offense, the defense. Soon, there was a cloud of dust, like Pig Pen[1], around the soccer ball with all the kids kicking at it. It's a wonder no one was seriously injured.

"What are you doing?" Coach Moore yelled to the goalie.

He swung on the horizontal part of the goalpost whenever the ball wasn't near him.

"Get your head in the game!"

Winning soccer for them was not a priority.

25

BARRY THE BIG MOUTH

W e often played poker in the morgue building. One night, my brother, Johnny, was visiting from Japan, and I tried to convince him to participate in a game.

"C'mon," I said. "It's only a friendly game. The most you win or lose is twenty bucks. Then, thinking of the grueling hours in the ER, I continued, "Besides, I need to unwind."

"I don't know about this," Johnny replied. "All those dead bodies give me the creeps. Maybe we should be more respectful."

"But they're dead. Harmless. You don't believe in ghosts, do you?"

"Of course not."

"Then, we can count you in?"

"Still, don't feel right."

I knew Johnny would accept it if I posed it as a challenge, so I played my Ace. "Sounds like you're afraid."

"Am not."

"Then you're in."

The game was with a surgical resident named Barry Brown, Dave (Barry's father), Dominic, and another resident named Harry. We called Barry "Big Mouth," because he was always bragging loudly. He even introduced himself as the burn doctor because, as a surgical resident, they debrided wounds of fire victims. In his green scrubs and stethoscope dangling around his neck, he was the picture of a doctor on call. He was pacing outside in the hallway.

"Expecting something?" I asked.

"One should always be prepared."

Johnny offered his hand. Barry ignored the gesture and said, "You're late."

"Wasn't it for 6:30?" I replied.

"No. It was for 6:15. You made us wait for fifteen minutes!" Barry said.

Then we stepped into a morgue room where the others were already sitting. A couple of cooled six-packs of beer awaited in a cooler.

"Well, it's about time you came," Dave, Barry's father, growled. He was the older image of Barry - short, with graying black hair. "It's cold in here!"

"Sorry."

"Saying 'Sorry' is not gonna give me back the fifteen minutes shivering in the cold," Barry snorted.

"It'll warm up once we start playing. Believe me."

"It better. Now sit down and play cards before I get frostbite."

With that, he took a wad of bills out and placed it on the table. So did his father. I looked at Johnny, who just shrugged. We only had about twenty dollars each.

"How much you got?" Barry asked.

"Enough. Why d'ya ask?"

"Because we want to make playing worth our while."

"Who says you're gonna win?

"I do."

Johnny just rolled his eyes.

"It's only nickel-dime-quarter[1] anyway," I said. "With a maximum of three raises."

"I know the game. Deal," Barry ordered.

I did after Dominic shuffled the cards. The body heat warmed up the room, so, it was a little chilly and not cold anymore.

"Give me a stiff one," Barry quipped.

"Very funny," I replied.

I passed him a can. We all gulped down our first.

"I'll raise a quarter," Barry said with a flair.

"But you haven't even looked at your cards," Dominic noted.

"Don't need to. I know they're good ones."

Again, Johnny rolled his eyes.

"What's the matter? You chicken?" Barry baited Johnny.

"Hey, he's our guest!" I reminded Barry.

"Meaning?"

"Meaning, cut him a little slack."

"Should I just give him my money because he's our 'guest?'"

"I'm in," Johnny said after peeking at his cards.

I looked at mine. *Ace, King, Queen, Jack, and seven. Guess I'll discard my seven and hope I draw a ten. That would give me a high straight.*

Dominic, Barry's father, and Harry all folded. It was Johnny and me against Barry.

He finally looked at his cards. With an obnoxious thud, he placed one card on the table.

"Gimme one good one," he said.

So, he's going for a straight, too. But if I get a ten, mine will be higher than his.

Johnny put down three cards. "Gimme three."

A pair is all he has.

I dealt the cards. I slowly looked at mine. It was a ten.

Sitting pretty.

Barry raised a quarter.

Got his card or bluffing. Either way, it's gonna feel really nice to see him lose.

"I'll see your quarter and raise you a quarter. I think you're bluffing."

"Oh yeah, we'll see who's bluffing. I see your quarter and raise it another quarter."

I threw the quarter into the pot[2]. It wasn't a lot of money, I just wanted to see Barry and his big mouth lose.

"Call," I said and revealed to him my cards. I took pleasure in putting the cards on the table. First, the ten. Then the King. I connected them with a Queen and Jack. Finally, I showed him my Ace. "Straight. Ace high."

I started to pull the pot toward me.

"Whoa! That's a good hand. But against me, that's not good enough. Read 'em and weep."

He also revealed his cards one at a time. Two fours and two fives. Going very slowly, he placed the fifth card on the table. It was a five. "Full boat. Five's over four's," he said, pulling the pot towards him.

The rest of the night was like that. Barry or his father won most pots. Johnny and I, lost our twenty dollars each. We finished off the six-packs as we played.

As we were leaving, Barry said in an exaggerated Southern drawl, "'Y'all come back now, y'hear.' I love taking your money, Johnny-Joe."

"Why you—"

Dominic stepped between us. "Go home and sleep it off before someone does something stupid."

A few nights later, I was home, trying to get used to sleeping at night after being on the night shift for a week. I awoke at about 3:00 a.m., wide awake, and couldn't get back to sleep. Rather than toss and turn and awaken Edie, I got up.

Now, what will I do? I know. Barry the Big Mouth is on call for surgery tonight. I'll call him.

I was not a Christian at the time and had never read the Bible. I knew I wanted revenge.

Time for payback.

I'm not proud of what I did. I only include the story to show what evil I can do. At the time, it may have seemed the right thing to do. However, deep down inside, I knew that it was wrong[3]. If anyone finds this story humorous, I suggest you check your own motives.

I dialed Barry's house.

"Hello?" he answered groggily. A baby cried in the background. Then another.

I put my hand over the receiver to disguise my voice.

"This is the ER. We have a surgical patient that needs evaluation for immediate surgery."

"I'll be right in."

When Barry arrived at the ER, no one knew what he was talking about. However, I subsequently learned he was married and had twins. My phone call had awakened them and his wife.

Can you imagine being married to a jerk like him?

Then came the voice of my conscience. *Correct me if I'm wrong, but didn't you wake her in the middle of the night? Who's the jerk here?*

I should've called him up to apologize, but I didn't.

26

THE CONFERENCE

Greg Cooney, another ER resident, and I went to California for a conference. He was carefree, but despite his prematurely balding head, was the picture of good health. At nearly six feet, he was almost as tall as me. Each year, the hospital sent the residents to a conference. It was an added perk. The real reason we went was for a vacation.

The sun was setting in San Francisco just as we arrived. It had been a long day of travel. We spent two hours driving to the airport, parking, boarding the plane, and then the five-hour flight. We were tired and signed in at the first motel we saw near the airport.

A clerk with pink hair didn't even look up at us. "One bed or two?" she asked.

At first, we thought she was joking and laughed. Then the clerk looked up and asked again, "One bed or two?"

"Give us two ... please," I muttered as seriously as possible.

We took the key and went to our room. I plopped on the bed without unpacking the bags. Greg turned out the light. I tried to fall asleep but had a difficult time with it. Half-awake, suddenly, the walls shook.

"What's going on?" I asked, switching on the light again.

"Just an earthquake."

"An earthquake! Shouldn't we do something?"

He laughed. "Yeah. Hope it's not the big one. Now, go to sleep."

He rolled over, and I turned out the light. Realizing he was right, I fell asleep.

In the morning, we had completely forgotten about the earthquake. We ate breakfast at a local diner, where we were seated and served promptly.

"I have a friend out here," Greg said as he ate some eggs. "Wanna see him?"

"Sure."

We checked in at the conference, then left to visit his friend. We were at the conference for maybe five minutes. No one would ever know the difference. Hey, at least we signed in!

We rendezvoused with Greg's friend Al, who showed us Oakland and Berkeley, where he lived. Al was a doctor, too. Afterward, he took us to his house, where we met his three roommates–two women and a man.

"Want some grass?" Terry, the middle-aged hippie man, said.

Greg and I were caught off-guard. However, that's the way they do things in California. People that hardly know you offer you marijuana.

"Why not?" Greg finally answered.

Don't wanna offend our hosts, I rationalized. So, we toked on a joint.

"Say, wanna go to the ballgame?" Al asked, after a while smoking the reefer.

Now any mention of baseball was an instant hit with me. "Sure."

He took us to the Oakland A's game against the White Sox.

The relief pitcher got hit with a batted ball in the ninth inning. Which team? I'm not sure. Who was winning? I didn't care. I had become both ignorant and apathetic.

"Should we run down on the field?" Greg asked. "After all, we are doctors."

While we hesitated, the pitcher got up and wasn't hurt, eliminating the need.

After dropping Al off and getting over the effects of the marijuana, Greg drove the rental car through Berkeley. *A Rocky Horror Picture Show* played at the cinema that night. The movie was just over, and the audience was spilling into the street. In the crowd were boots, chains, and other paraphernalia. The pedestrians were dressed up to mirror the people on the screen.

"What's that?" Greg pointed to a man dressed totally in leather with a whip.

"Just ignore him and keep driving."

"This is plain crazy!"

"It's normal for California."

The next day we were off to Napa Valley for a wine tasting tour. Some of the wineries I had boycotted years before were now serving free wine. Greg and I couldn't resist. The boycott was over anyway. I don't know how wine connoisseurs do it without getting drunk. By the end of the day, we indeed were a little tipsy. And we were driving! Again, not too smart a thing to do.

"Wanna go to Yosemite while we're in the neighborhood?" Greg asked.

Neighborhood! Yosemite was 200 miles away! However, I remembered El Capitan and Half Dome's spectacular beauty from thirteen years ago.

"Does a duck like water? It's better than any conference," I said.

We left for Yosemite. Greg and I climbed Half Dome again, taking the same route I took in 1969. The water thundered over Nevada Falls like a giant faucet. Flowers of all colors were everywhere, dotting the countryside. Nothing had changed.

Beautiful!

Greg and I climbed up and down Jacob's Ladder. After we came down it to the forest, there were wavy lines through my vision. It only lasted a few minutes. It was a premonition of things to come. However, I ignored it and hoped it would go away.

"Look over there," Greg pointed.

Two bare-breasted women were hiking. The wavy lines disappeared as I gaped.

Everything in California is different.

We continued our hike down. When we reached the bottom, we drove to San Francisco, where we saw men holding each other's hands and kissing in broad daylight. The usually carefree Greg stopped suddenly, his mouth open, and said, "Will you look at that?"

"I'd rather not."

Yes, California *is* different.

We flew home. Back in Danville, I unpacked. Then I noticed a brown paper bag stashed in my gear.

What's this?

I opened it to see another bag filled with sensimilla[1] marijuana.

How did that get there?

Then I realized that Greg had stashed it in *my* gear.

I saw red.

If the airport police had stopped us, I would've gone to jail and lost my license! It's a good thing we weren't. Have to give it to Greg tomorrow.

27

APPENDICITIS

Shortly after our return from California, my abdomen started hurting one night, so I called the hospital.

"Who's on for surgery?"

"Dr. Price," the nurse answered.

Oh, great! I thought facetiously. *Don't like how he operates, even if he is the Chief of Surgery. I'll wait until morning when the shift changes.*

My abdomen hurt worse. I couldn't sit quietly any longer.

It might burst if I wait too long!

So, I walked to the hospital around the corner. With each step, I reached for my right side.

Must be bad. I'm guarding.

Larry Sherwood, the ER Doc who took Bob Bagley's place, evaluated me.

"Hmm," he said, "looks like appendicitis. But I have good news for you, Dr. Price is on."

Why is he still on? Oops, I forgot. It's Friday night. He'll be on all weekend. But I took consolation in thinking, *the residents will do the surgery anyway. No worry.*

Dr. Price arrived shortly after that and evaluated me. Afterward, he insisted, "I'll do the surgery. No need to call a resident."

That's not what I wanted to hear. But it's only an appendectomy. Even I can do that.

Then Dr. Price left for the OR. He left me alone for a moment behind the pull curtains separating me from the next gurney.

What can I do? Leave? No, I can't do that. The appendix has to come out before I really get into trouble. I'm done for.

Then, Dr. Sherwood opened one of the curtains and looked at my monitor. "You went into bigeminy[1]. You're flipping a lot of PVCs[2]. Don't worry about the surgery. It's a piece of cake."

*I know it is. Even I did one. No, I'm not worried about the surgery at all. I'm worried about **who** is doing it!*

Our foster son, Jimmy, was the orderly on duty. He prepped me and placed a Foley catheter to eliminate my urine, hooking it up to a bag on my leg. It was strange to me to have our son shave my belly and put in a catheter.

Another rite of passage.

I settled into the gurney. Unfortunately, it was hard and made waiting difficult.

What's taking so long?

I became impatient.

Maybe that's why they call us "patients!"

I laughed, but that caused pain in my right side. I grimaced.

"Don't laugh," the nurse advised me.

Now they tell me.

When the orderly final took me to the OR, I don't remember anything. I mean, I was out in a flash. The anesthesiologist put me under. I don't even remember the way *to* the surgery.

I was in the hospital and treated royally for two days. Then, they discharged me home for further recovery. During that time, I was supposed to urinate on my own. When I tried, something unusual to me blocked me up.

What's in there?

Then I peed some air.

How did that get there? Dr. Price hooked up my bowel to my bladder somehow. He fouled up my insides!

So, I went back to the ER.

I knew I should have left before he touched me, I thought as I lay on the same gurney from before. Skins pulled the curtains and entered my little cubicle.

"I have good news," he said while holding my chart. "The air is from the Foley insertion. Now take advantage of the time off before you enter the real world."

Whew! Dodged a bullet. This being a patient is not so bad. It's good that this happened now and not afterward when we moved.

So, I enjoyed the end of my residency because I was recovering. When I could, I visited my parents, leaving Edie at home with the kids. We were used to separate vacations. I wanted to be there when Johnny came home from Japan and meet him at my parents' house. He came home every June and helped around the house until mid-August. He always claimed that there were three good reasons to have a career in teaching. "June, July, and August."

Anyway, my father was now seventy and retired from being an editor at Prentice-Hall. Growing up, I remember he brought home a typewriter they would throw away. The "l" key stuck. In effect, it was missing an "l." We called it 'The Christmas Typewriter—No-el."

DAD WORKED part-time as a ranger at a local golf course. Mostly he planted flowers on the tees. "I'm the original Flower Child," he often quipped.

He got us on the golf course for a reduced fee–peanuts really. I had to cut down on my swing because I didn't want to tear anything.

Actually, this improves my game.

28

MERCY HOSPITAL

E die and I had to decide where to go once my residency was over. Where was the best place to raise our family?

I took a protractor and drew a circle with a sixty-mile radius on a map, and Port Jervis, NY, at the center. We could live anywhere in it. The circle was close enough to my parents, sister, and New York City for a day trip by car. Northeastern Pennsylvania was near Edie's parents, too. Scranton was on the perimeter—Wilkes-Barre, too far.

I wrote to all the hospitals in that circle to see if they needed anybody—fishing for work. The only response I got was from Peter Lynch in Scranton, who coordinated the ER, or dispensary as it was called, at Mercy Hospital there. He was the brother of the nun who ran it. Peter had a full head of gray hair, was about six feet tall, and was fit. He had the gift of gab.

"Being of Irish descent, we think the poor should be cared for," Peter said. "You'll be the medical director of the ER someday. We'll start you off at $70,000[1]."

That was what I wanted to hear. I thought then that money was important.

$70,000 is a lot of money. They must like me.

"My mother's maiden name is Kelly," I said.

"I know."

"How'd you know that?"

"It's my job to know," he replied, then continued, "Actually, it's on your application. That's why I called you. You'll fit right in."

Peter drove me about nine miles to the suburbs of Scranton to a huge hill at the bottom of Clarks Summit. We went under a towering bridge.

"What's that?" I asked.

"The Pennsylvania Turnpike. It ends in the hills here."

"Wow! That's a high bridge. I'd hate to drive over it."

The Turnpike went over the hills to Wilkes-Barre. I didn't know then that in ten years it would play a big part in my life.

Clarks Summit, was country but still had the main street with shops. I was impressed.

"This is where all the doctors live. Good schools here through high school. Even have a college up one of the hills."

"There is? I thought I knew all the colleges around here. What's it called?"

"Not sure. It's a Bible Seminary for Southern Baptists, and we're Catholics. What denomination are you?"

"I had twelve years of Catholic school, so I guess I'm a Catholic. But I'm not very religious. Is that important?"

"Not really. It's just that I wouldn't tell Sister that."

"When can I meet her?"

"Later today. Let me show you more of Clarks Summit. Then we can go to lunch. After that, we'll meet Sister Claire William."

So, Peter showed me around Clarks Summit, which was typical suburbia. There were well-trimmed lawns, plenty of trees, wooden houses with fiberglass siding – not too ornate. I didn't see any of the brick and concrete buildings I was used to.

Yep. Can raise a family here.

We finally headed back toward Scranton and Mercy Hospital.

"Where do you live?" I asked.

"Scranton."

"Why not Clarks Summit?"

"Can't afford it."

"Oh," I said apologetically.

We stopped at Cooper's restaurant, where they had the best Lobster Newberg. Afterward, he took me to meet Sister Claire William.

Peter left me alone in her office. The light was dim on her mahogany desk. Books lined the walls on bookcases. I sank into a plush, leather chair across from the desk. I started to get nervous.

Feel like I'm back in grade school at the Mother Superior's office.

Miss Black, her secretary, came in and said, "Sister has been unavoidably detained. I'm so sorry. Do you want some tea while we wait?"

I didn't want to offend her hospitality, so I replied, "Why not?"

She left and came back with a cup. Steam rose from the brew. I could only think of Carly Simon's line, "Clouds in my coffee."

But this is tea!

I sipped some and waited.

Finally, Sister Claire made her grand entrance. She was a little woman and thin.

"I'm so sorry," she apologized, "but I had to attend to something. Busy, busy, busy. There is not enough time in the day."

I was taken aback by the habit she wore or, should I say, lack of one. She wore a standard business suit–a white blouse, gray jacket, and skirt. The only part of her apparel that identified her as a nun was her blue and white cap. Having been raised by nuns and taking care of them as a resident, I was immediately deferential.

"Sister, it's good of you to see me."

She sat behind her colossal desk. I had trouble seeing her from my chair.

"Tell me about yourself," Sister Claire said as she settled into her chair behind the desk.

She had a way about her that I hadn't witnessed since Cesar Chavez—disarming.

I spoke for about an hour. Then she said, "Mercy Hospital system is a big one. Second only to the VA in the US. We have four hospitals in Pennsylvania. Our benefits and retirement plan are second to none." She paused and let that information percolate before continuing, "We must keep up with the times. Don't want to die on the vine. I promise you that you will be director someday," Sister assured me.

My Catholic upbringing resurfaced. It never crossed my mind that a nun would mislead me. The fact she was Irish-American also helped to convince me, too.

I'm finally out on my own in the real world.

I didn't feel GOD's directing hand. I was like a fish in a milk bottle, too stupid to turn around.

We rose and shook hands. Then Sister ushered me out of her office The glitz had blinded me.

On the way home, I kept thinking, *It looks like Scranton.*

29

BUYING THE NEW HOUSE

Now that my residency was over, Edie and I needed a house. We had never owned one before.

"I'm so excited!" she said. "Hurry up and get dressed. We're supposed to meet the Realtor."

I did and we drove to the parking lot where we were to meet the Realtor.

After a half hour waiting, the Realtor still hadn't shown up.

"Do we have the right place?" I asked.

Edie was fidgety, but managed to reply, "She said to meet her at the McDonald's. That's where we are."

"Do you know how many McDonald's there are?"

Refusing to consider the obvious, Edie said, "She must've got caught in traffic."

We waited for another half hour. No Realtor. This was before the advent of cell phones or a GPS, so we finally left and went back to Danville.

As we walked through the doorway, the telephone rang and Edie went to answer it. The phone was in the kitchen and I was two rooms away in the living room. All I could hear was Edie's voice mumbling something. Finally, the conversation ended and Edie came back to the living room.

"Who was that?" I asked.

"The Realtor. We had the wrong McDonald's. We'll try again tomorrow."

"*We* will? I was supposed to play golf tomorrow."

"Cancel."

"Just like that?"

She nodded. "This is really important."

"How do you know my golf isn't?"

"Look, I've waited all these years for this. I can see where your priorities are."

"You never once asked me who I was playing with."

"I don't care if it's the pope. We need a house."

"What about the kids?"

"The Simonds can babysit them again. It's about *the kids'* future, too."

Now, there was no arguing with her. Besides, I hated to admit it, but she was right. I got on the phone and called Peter Lynch. We exchanged pleasantries then I said, "I can't play tomorrow."

"Why?"

"House-hunting."

"That's great! I have some things I need to get done around here anyway. This is better."

So, we met with the Realtor. She was a tall, thin, woman named Ashley Combs. She offered me her hand. I shook it vigorously.

"We finally meet," Ashley said. "Sorry about the mix-up yesterday."

"It wasn't your fault."

"Let me drive because I know the roads."

We readily agreed and got in her car.

"I have just the place for you. It's a great starter home. The backyard ends at the high school property, so no one can ever build there. One house down is a road that goes through the woods and is perfect for walking. Not much traffic."

We drove under the towering bridge. Edie's eyes grew wide, but remained silent.

Then we motored up the huge hill on the highway and arrived in Clarks Summit. We pulled off the main road onto another one that ran perpendicular to it. There were many twists and turns.

"It's a good thing you're driving," I said. "We never would have found it."

"Almost there," Ashley replied.

Finally, we turned off that onto another street. It was almost dizzying, but it was also private. Woods were on the right and an open field on the left.

"The house is down the end of this street," Ashley said while making one more turn onto Welsh Hill Road. Near the end, we pulled into a driveway of a split-level home.

Edie poked me in the ribs and whispered, "I like it already."

Ashley showed us the house. With three bedrooms, two rooms downstairs, a garage beneath the second level, the living room, dining room, and kitchen. It was big enough.

Then we went outside. The back had an open-air elevated porch beneath which tools were stored. It was connected to the kitchen. There was a huge back yard. On either side were tall pine trees that gave a sense of privacy. Across a ditch, the end abutted against high school property.

When we returned to the car, Ashley asked, "Well, what do you think?"

"How much?" I asked.

"That's the best part. Only $66,000."

I scratched my chin. Edie nudged me. I said, "Sounds good. We have to talk a little about it, though. Can I get back to you?"

"Don't take too long. That house is a steal."

When Ashley dropped us off at our car, as soon as the door was closed, Edie said, "I love the house! Call her as soon as we get home."

"$66,000 is a lot of money."

"Not for us it isn't. Think big."

"I'll offer $63,000 and see if it's accepted."

As soon as we got to our home in Danville, I called Ashley.

"We want to make an offer," I told her.

"Great! How much?"

"$63,000."

"I'll get back to you to see if they accept."

After I hung up, Edie tugged on my sleeve.

"I *really* want that house," she said. "Now is not a time to be cheap."

We waited for the phone to ring. In about an hour it did. It was Ashley.

"Well?" I asked.

"They said they'd sell it for $64,500. That's a final offer."

"We'll take it!"

"Great! You can come to my office for the closing and get the keys. Congratulations! You're going to be the new owner of the house."

And that's what we did. I had a new job and a new house. Things were looking as if our ship had finally come in.

30

SETTLING IN

T he house was ours.

When we married, we could move all our stuff in one carload. Now, we needed a big truck. By this time, we were experts in moving, having moved twelve times in eleven years. However, no matter how often you move, it is still stressful.

"This goes in that box," Edie said, lifting a bowl for nuts I had put with the towels.

"It's fragile. I got it from my mother. I put it there on purpose, so the towels cushioned it."

"But it's a knick-knack and belongs with the other knick-knacks. Otherwise, it could get lost."

"But—" I started and caught myself before I said something stupid, which I was prone to do.

No matter what you say, a voice from inside me advised, *you're not gonna win this argument. Drop it now! Besides, it **is** only a knick-knack and not worth fighting about.*

"Tell you what. Why don't we put all the knick-knacks in with the towels and that way, nothing can break?" I said.

"Now, you're talking."

We did just that and avoided an argument. It would've led to us not speaking to each other. Both of us were very stubborn. We'd been down that road for weeks at a time before. Neither of us wanted to do it again. The stress of moving was enough.

The old saw says, "behind every good man, there is a good woman." That was true in my case. Yes, we had our problems, but we worked them out. It was generally a good marriage. Maybe Edie was a tad much into woman's lib, but I lived with it. After all, I'm not the easiest person to live with, either. I didn't know how good I had it. Then Valerie re-entered the story. But I'm getting ahead of myself again.

The movers came with the truck. Jimmy stayed in Danville, where he had his own place. The other three kids piled into the back of our rusty Nova. Then we took off like Abram and Sarai going to Canaan. To us, Clarks Summit was the Promised Land.

After the two-hour ride, we finally pulled into the driveway of our new home. I forgot that I had applied Rustoleum over the years to cover patches of rust. At the time, I thought Rustoleum only came in one color and that it changed yearly. I learned too late that we could buy it in matching colors anytime. As a result, assorted mismatched colors - primarily browns and grays - covered the once-gold Nova from where I had applied it over different years.

When he saw us arrive, eight-year-old Louis Krueger, the oldest kid of the neighbors across the street, screamed while holding his mother's hand, "Look, Mommy, they're in the army!"

"Shh!"

"But the car is camouflaged. Are we supposed to see it?"

"They're not in the army. Let's go inside." And they disappeared.

We entered our new house. You could go upstairs to the living room or downstairs to the children's playroom and the garage. There was a railing on the landing over the foyer where you came inti the house.

ABOUT A YEAR LATER, Edie admitted, "I don't like it."

"Why not?"

She pointed to where it extended into the living room. "See that? So does everyone else. I don't think guests should have a view of our living room when they come in. Who knows how we'll be dressed or what we'll be doing?"

"Aren't you exaggerating a little bit?"

"Am I?" Edie replied coquettishly.

So, I built a wall where the railing was to separate the living room from the downstairs. I painted it, but the seam showed. I papered the wall, but the crack was still visible. Finally, I decided on fancy plywood.

"The carpet doesn't match the wall," Edie grumbled.

"Why not?"

"Too light."

So, I bought a gray rug that was the same color. Shannon christened it by vomiting on it.

"The new carpet doesn't match the other walls!" Edie exclaimed.

"Why not?

"Too dark."

So, the entire upstairs was altered, taking the wallpaper off with a rented steamer. What started as one wall eventually included the whole house!

We were relaxing against an unpainted wall one night, when Edie, looking at me with her big brown eyes said, "It would be so-o much easier to keep clean if you used oil-based paint."

What could I do? I surrendered and painted the wall. But what did I know? I was a novice with oil-based paint. Everything was fine until I tried to clean the brushes.

"The paint won't come off!" I exclaimed in the bathroom. "It's making a mess!"

"You didn't try to clean them with water, did you?"

"Wasn't I supposed to?"

"Even I know that you don't! Didn't you read the can?"

"No," I admitted like a boy who caught his hand in the cookie jar. "Now, what do I do?"

"Try turpentine!"

That worked.

Our failure to see each other's point of view went way beyond paint. Edie was dissatisfied being a doctor's wife, whatever that is. She returned to school, enrolling in a college nearby named Marywood. At first, Edie took arts and crafts courses. I thought she would use some of the money I earned as a doctor to open a store in Clarks Summit, so I supported the idea. However, school diminished her time with the kids and me.

Then, Edie selected business courses without consulting me. I should have objected, but I didn't.

A woman needs to have her own life and not be defined by a man. The market for morality is open to all. Aren't we all equal?

I thought that was how it was because we made it that way. Now, I realize we're equal because of GOD[1].

Then, Jimmy got into trouble driving drunk and lost his license after we left Danville. He moved in with us again. I split the two-car garage and made it a room for him.

Even with him there, I insisted on doing the yard work.

Maybe that will keep me in shape.

However, we had a big backyard with pines on either side and an open middle area. After mowing it a few times, all thoughts of staying in shape evaporated. It became a chore.

Who invented lawns anyway?

When I used a rake and shovel to clear the rear garden, black liquid oozed up from the ground.

Oil! I thought and entertained visions of Jed Clampett's[2]'s bonanza.

I went inside and exclaimed to Edie, "This house is a gold mine! We're sitting on a huge lake of oil!"

She must have some Missouri blood in her because Edie said skeptically, "Show me."

So, I led her by the hand to the black liquid that oozed from the ground.

She laughed. "That's not oil. This whole yard is a big drainage field for the house. The overflow from the septic tank goes into it. Whenever we have a good rain, like we had a few nights ago, it overflows. You hit some of it! Didn't you know that? Didn't you ever wonder why the garden grows so well?"

"How do you know so much?" I asked, impressed.

"Having a father who's an electrician helps."

Lucky it wasn't a lot worse.

I returned to pruning the garden, this time more carefully. Edie went back to the house.

Beyond the ditch was the high school track. Below one end was a hill, where I took the kids sledding. At the opposite end was the north campus of the high school, where the juniors and seniors went.

Because the house was a split-level, there was no place to escape the noise of the kids. Edie had a hard time when I worked nights.

"Shh! Daddy's sleeping," she repeated many times.

But it was a losing battle, and kids make noise. Their function is to disrupt their parents' lives.

31

PATRICK MCCARTHY

While at the house on Welsh Hill, I maintained my friendship with Patrick McCarthy.

One weekend, Pat visited with his lady friend, Bev Barr. They stayed over Friday night.

Early Saturday morning, eight-year-old Josh, still in his pajamas, woke us up as the sun rose and said, "What's Pat doing in the backyard?"

I got up after putting on some clothes and looked out the window. Pat was in the backyard dressed in a black pajama outfit and barefoot. His arms and legs appeared to cut the air in slow motion.

"Practicing karate," I answered as if everybody did.

"What's car-ati?

"Not car-ati. Karate. Judo."

Now how do you explain that to a kid?

I fell back on the time-honored explanation. "You'll understand when you get older. Now, go back to bed."

Did I just say that? I sound like my parents. Maybe their parents said the same to them when they were kids. If you don't know the answer, say, "Don't bother me," or something like I just did.

I had never seen my parents as inquisitive kids themselves before. I shuddered.

Josh shrugged it off, and he and I went back to sleep. Edie had barely moved.

I wanted Pat's opinion of the trial scene in *Journey of the Peacemakers* because he's a lawyer. Then the book was called, *Candles in the Rain*, a novel I was writing at the time. So, after breakfast, Bev read all sixty pages of it. Since then, I've cut it way down.

When she had finished, I asked, "Well, what do you think?"

"Very interesting."

An author's ego is very fragile.

But not "good." Can learn more from what a person doesn't say than from what they do. Guess I have to re-write it.

With her dark eyes and hair, Bev resembled Edie. They could have passed for sisters, even twins. She was an artist and had a teenage daughter named Janine. Pat moved in with her and shared expenses in her New Jersey house.

She planned a surprise fortieth birthday party for Pat and invited Edie and me. I made a tape of the basketball game with "Shoot, McCarthy, Shoot," saying it was from our grammar school days over twenty-five years before and had found it by accident when moving. No one believed it because tape players were not popular then. When I started to play the tape at his party, they heard the crowd. I had enlisted my kids, all four of them, plus Edie, to be the background noise while I narrated the story. Now, I had introduced just enough doubt that people became quiet and listened.

"He shot before getting to mid-court," I announced in the middle of the tape. "Time stood still as the ball left his hands. For a moment, the crowd was hushed … "

The kids and Edie were silent for a moment.

" … The ball flew through the air and went toward the basket. But it kept going past it and above the backboard. It ricocheted off the stanchions and went out the open window! The ball bounced down the walkway and tripped the mailman!"

The kids and Edie started to laugh in the background.

I gave Pat the tape and a book *he* had loaned *me* as a birthday present. We had wrapped the book in paper. When he opened it, he said, "Hey, this looks familiar."

Of course, it did! It was his book!

Then it dawned on him what I'd done. Pat laughed while muttering, "I'll get you for this."

He got his chance a couple of months later, on *my* fortieth birthday. Pat produced a video in which he interviewed different people about me, including my parents. He plugged it into our VCR[1] with all my friends there. Sitting at a desk, Pat came up, claiming, "I want to thank Joe Thek for bringing to my friends' attention my prowess on the basketball court. I said I hoped I could repay the favor. So, I produced this tape. It revealed a side of Joe Thek that I never knew existed. Quite frankly, it startled me. So, for the next half hour, sit back and see this series of interviews about the life and times of Joe Thek."

Then we were transported to my parent's living room. Mom and Dad were sitting on the sofa. "He was the reason the Dodgers left Brooklyn," Dad claimed. "Joey would yell profanity at the players from the stands. Even when he was a little boy."

Mom sat there quietly while Dad rambled on. "The night I remember most was Gate Night[2] one year. Joey was brought home by the police. The policeman had him by the scruff of his jacket. He had thrown a water balloon at a moving car and knocked off his side mirror. I don't know why they didn't arrest him for being a hooligan. It would have saved us all those police lights. What an embarrassment! Who knows what the neighbors thought?"

Pat then interviewed a man in combat fatigues, who allegedly was General Maury Chavez.

"He told his friends that he went to California. But he really went to Vietnam," he began while twirling an arrow in his hands. "We called him 'The Palmster' because he loved napalm. He loved ice cream even more. Once, he traded napalm for a couple gallons of Carvel ice cream."

"Is this the right, Joe Thek?" Pat asked.

"Of course, it's the right Joe Thek!" General Chavez retorted. "How many Joe Theks do you know?" Then he started drinking a clear fluid.

"Now, calm down. Calm down. Joe told us that he went to

California to do his peace thing with Cesar Chavez and the farm workers."

"Ha! He went to California all right, to Chavez Ravine, where the Dodgers play in LA. That crazy *#*# gets thrown out for swearing at the Dodgers. Then he enlists in the army under me, General Chavez." He took another swig.

After laughing, he continued, "I'll tell you something else about Thek. He liked the ladies. He hated doctors at the M*A*S*H unit in 'Nam, too. "There was only one thing that could get him to a M*A*S*H unit—a nurse. Thek, loved this Nubian queen and always came back. He fathered a black girl while there."

"Can I ask what you're drinking?"

"Vodka."

"Vodka! It's only ten in the morning!"

"Calms my nerves." And with that, he turned the arrow again.

"Do you have anything to say to Joe?"

"No … on second thought, yes. Would he like to go back to Laos? Special Forces could use a crazy *#*# like, Thek."

Then Pat lampooned me as a doctor. He took us to an alleged meeting of my former ER patients, that were all supposedly involved in a class action suit against me. A man and a woman sat on opposite ends of a sofa. He says, "A laughing Doctor Thek examined my twisted ankle. The next thing I know, I go off to surgery for Open Heart Surgery."

"What happened to your ankle?" Pat asks.

"As you can see it's still swollen. Because I sit around a lot, I eat. I've put on fifty pounds. All due to Doctor—Thek."

Then a boy with a deformed shoulder comes in and sits by the woman.

"Who's he?" Pat asks.

"My son, Ralph."

"I see his shoulder is off. Tell me your story."

"It was only a bee sting, but Ralph is allergic. This doctor comes into the room wearing a Brooklyn Dodgers baseball cap."

He says, "If you want me to see your son, you'll have to do me a favor."

"What's that?"

"You have to sleep with me. I couldn't believe it. And my son right there."

"Why, that's terrible," Pat says.

"He never did take care of his arm, and you can see where that's led."

They were compelling. I don't know where Pat found them.

Then the scene switched to an interview with a young black woman.

"Can you tell us your name?"

"Tina—Tina Thek."

"If you don't mind me saying so, that's not a black name."

"I'm Joe Thek's daughter. This weekend I'm coming to see him."

Finally, Pat videoed Edie.

"While Joe's been running around having all these affairs, I've had a lover of my own," she averred. "Wanna see him?"

Edie held a picture up to the camera. It was of me in a clown mask. We had a good laugh. I guess turnabout is fair play.

32

IAN O'GRADY

Once I finished my residency, my compadre, Ian O'Grady, took me up to his cottage[1] in upstate New York to winterize [2]it every November around Veteran's Day. We drove to the North Country up a lonely Route 81, stopping at a McDonald's along the way to catch a bite to eat.

The thing I remember most about the North Country was how gray and desolate everything was. The sky was gray. The leafless trees were gray. Even the wooden houses were gray. The cars were mostly dark-colored to capture the heat of the sun. Structures were built on the gray rock. It was everywhere. We explored the area on drives and saw stone walls by each house. The only thing white was the big satellite TV dishes before each house. Everybody had satellite TV. It didn't matter if you lived in a shack; you had a dish in front of the house. We saw these giant monstrosities acting as status symbols in the middle of nowhere. It seemed each person wanted to get one bigger than their neighbor.

We finally got to his camp by turning off the paved road down a long dirt lane through the woods. The branches of the trees hung down and obscured the view of where we were going. As hidden as it was, you would never have known there was a trail unless you had been on it. How they ever found the camp, I'll never know.

IT WAS good to get away and return to the place I had visited as a teenager. Across the lake was the cliff from which Ian and I jumped in our teen years. The constant northwest wind had bent the pines. Nothing had changed.

The camp lacked heat and a bathroom. It boasted an outhouse and was cold. We roughed it for three or four days. Our hair was unkempt, and our faces unshaven. But who cared?

I remember Ian's scaly hands. The cold must have affected them badly. However, he never complained about them. He just wore gloves to prevent them from cracking. He treated it as just a part of life.

Ian had fixed it up on the inside. He had a fundamental skill in making things out of what some people would think of as garbage. But he made everything fit together. There were two bedrooms on the porch and two small ones inside. I slept on the lower bunk bed in one. The kitchen was narrow, but long. If one wanted to wash dishes, one filled a pot with water from the lake, heated it on the gas stove, and then poured the hot water into a plastic basin in the sink. Nothing was easy.

Eventually, Ian made an indoor shower with hot water. I don't know how he did it, just that he did.

A pot-bellied stove stood in the main room of the camp. We always made a fire in it with wood that Ian had chopped the previous summer. We started the blaze with the paper from the local newspaper. The stove made the camp livable. It was quite a chore to get up in the frigid morning to start it.

An antique and battered hutch held dishes. They were old and mismatched but served us well. Shelves with books occupied other walls. Ian and I used to eat and play chess at a table that held court over the main room. It was a multi-purpose table – serving for meals, playing chess, or just chatting. A couple of couches and chairs invited lounging. Ian loved fixing old radios at a desk covered with odd parts and tubes.

There was no phone. That's an instant priority – an interruption. If you wanted contact with the outside world, you called from Hubert Cole's house in nearby Plessis. Hubert ran the post office out of his house. He was an elderly man with gnarled fingers and hands. Hubert read things with a magnifying glass. Ian knew him because, when Hubert was younger, he owned the camp next to Ian's.

"Judas Priest," he'd say, "I remember the days of The Prohibition when bootleggers would deliver liquor in trucks from Canada over the frozen St. Lawrence. The G-men would chase 'em. They'd skedaddle like spiders do when someone turns on the light. We hid them in barns until the coast was clear."

Ian and I went drinking and driving then (don't tell anyone) on dirt, back roads. His car had a four-wheel drive and went nearly anywhere. He had a CB radio in the vehicle in case we were lost, which happened frequently. As I said, Ian liked radios. Having one accessible in the car made him feel at ease.

Every time we went to the North Country, something went wrong: the pump froze, the car ran out of gas, or it got stuck in the mud. Something unusual would always happen. You could depend on it.

"I want to see some local color," I said one evening as we sat at the table after shaving and taking a shower in the new bathroom. The sun was setting over the lake casting long shadows on the water.

"Are you sure?"

"Yeah. How else can I write about it?"

"Then grab your coat and come on. I'll show you some 'local color.'"

Ian and Hubert in Pleases, Upstate New York

HE TOOK me to a bar in the nearby town of Teresa. As we entered, a man toted out a woman on his shoulder. I should've turned around, but I was curious.

One fiery, red-haired woman hit another blonde woman in the face, and then a man carried the red-haired woman out by her hair.

"I went to a bar once, and a fight broke out," Ian began. "Before I knew it, bottles and chairs were flying everywhere. I left. Then the bar caught on fire and burned right to the ground. The police arrived and arrested people. The owners never rebuilt."

What am I getting into now?

We visited the Flat Rock bar in Plessis, New York. They had a one-armed bouncer and a pool table, and I liked to play. So, I asked a young man at the bar, "Do you wanna play?"

"Me?" he asked and pointed to his chest.

I nodded, and he picked up a cue stick from the table and put a quarter down for a little bet on the game. We didn't mean it to be a lot of money. I had learned from my years at the caddy shack that you shouldn't get involved in big money. You either lose your money or, if you win, you lose your friends because some of them don't pay. Besides, you never know when your opponent will get angry or if he has a weapon.

We played eight-ball. After the break, I ran a couple of balls, then missed. My opponent only needed one miscue because he ran the table and picked up the quarter. GOD must have been with me because I had lost and left the table. He challenged another fellow to a game.

Ian poked me on the shoulder, "Move to the end of the bar."

"Why?"

"Just do it."

After I did, I asked, "Why does the bouncer only have one arm?"

"You'll see."

The young man I'd been playing with hit his opponent over the head with his cue stick. I thought all heck would break loose. I had visions of broken mirrors and flying chairs. But the bouncer controlled the situation like it was an everyday occurrence. He calmly drew a gun out of his coat with one arm and pointed it at the instigator.

"That'll be it, right there," the bouncer said. "Now vamoose," and he tilted his head toward the door.

"B—"

The bouncer clicked the hammer back with his one thumb.

"I'm goin', I'm goin'!" the young man said hurriedly and left.

Hmm! Glad I lost!

Adjoining the bar was a dance hall, and we entered and sat. A blonde floozy sidled up and asked Ian, "Would you like to dance?"

"Sure."

After one dance, they left the establishment, deserting me in this dangerous place.

Soon, a young lady with two brothers flanking her approached me. "Wanna dance?"

I wanted to reply, *"What is it about this place? Aren't the men supposed to ask the women to dance?"* But seeing her brothers, I replied, "Okay."

She had "summer teeth." (Some were there, and some weren't.)

While dancing, I wondered, *Where is Ian?*

The lady and I use the term loosely, asked, "Why don't you come home with me?"

Looking at her two big brothers, I thought, *They'll beat me to a pulp if I say "No!" Where is Ian anyway? How do I get out of this in one piece?*

Tiny beads of sweat appeared on my brow.

Think! Think! What am I gonna do?

My forte is not usually thinking quickly. However, on this occasion, I blurted out the first thought I had.

"Say, want a beer?" I asked the brothers avoiding her question.

They had found a pigeon to pay for their drinks. The brothers had me in a stranglehold and were not about to let go.

I didn't even know her name. The lady says, "Well?"

"I'm married."

"That's great! So am I!"

Oh great! Where is Ian? There's no telling where this lady has been.

One brother comes to my aid. "Leave him alone. I'm thirsty."

"Yeah, let us drink up," the other brother says.

With that, she says, "Then fill her up!"

I couldn't believe it! If paying for their drinks would save my skin, I got away cheap.

After a couple of drinks, they were plastered, and Ian returned from somewhere outside.

Now to get out of here.

Everybody was drunk except for us. I was too scared to drink, and Ian was busy watching everybody else.

Then it was time for the bar to close. Ian grabbed my arm and said, "Wait!"

We hurried to the end of the table while everyone left, including the lady and her two brothers. We watched through the window as all the patrons piled into their pick-up trucks. The vehicles plowed over front lawns, garbage cans, and bushes like bumper cars. It's a wonder no one was hurt.

"I've seen enough local color," I said nervously. "Can we go now?"

Ian nodded. We silently drove back to the camp. Ian had shown me what "local color" meant. It frightened me.

I STILL PURSUED that elusive first principle, the bedrock from which everything else is derived. It's there as long as one doesn't give up looking. We stumble like drunks in pick-ups playing bumper cars and running over garbage cans. Some will deny that HE exists–including us at that time. As I age and gain more experience, HE becomes obvious. Why didn't I see HIM sooner? GOD had HIS reasons for HIS apparent disguise. I'm just glad I finally did see.

33

BILL AGAIN

While visiting with Pat McCarthy and Ian O'Grady, Bill Ranetsky and I kept in contact. I saw him in Pittsburgh several times.

One afternoon after his work, we were on the way to Bill's parent's house to visit his boys. Suddenly, he pulled off the road.

"Why are we stopping?"

"To play *Asteroid* at the arcade," he said, almost drooling at the prospect, wiping his dark hair with a streak of gray out of his eyes.

"But Jason (Bill's oldest boy) has a cello performance tonight!"

"We have time."

"You're addicted to computer games."

We played a game at the arcade, then stopped to pick up his son.

"You need to get your priorities straight," I muttered before we entered his parent's house.

"You need to keep your opinions to yourself."

Did he just tell me to shut up?

We glared at each other but were speechless temporarily. However, neither one of us can stay angry for very long. In about an hour, while listening to Jason play the cello beautifully, we had forgotten the whole thing.

BILL MET AND DATED MARY. They became serious and eventually purchased a house together in East McKeesport, outside Pittsburgh.

"Have to see if we're compatible," he explained.

"What if you're not?"

"Split up."

"Just like that? You don't work it out?"

"Can't. We're both set in our ways."

I looked skeptically at him, but he refused to acknowledge that people can change.

Then Bill bought a dog named Chauncey. He was a Springer Spaniel, brown and white, with big adorable eyes and floppy ears. Chauncey loved to jump, mostly on me.

"Chauncey has fleas," Bill announced one evening.

"No wonder my ankles itch."

"I have to gas the house with a flea bomb."

"Don't let me stop you."

Bill fumigated the house. We couldn't move out the furniture because that's where the fleas lived. We had to stay outside while the flea bomb worked. It was a minor inconvenience.

While we waited, we needed a distraction. Looking around, Mary, who loved to grow flowers, pointed to her latest bumper crop next to the house and asked me, "What kind of flowers are these?"

The question caught me off guard, so I replied, "Red and blue ones."

She laughed, then said, "They're Impatiens and Morning Glory. C'mon. We'll go to the Botanical Gardens and teach you some names."

We went there, but I never learned.

READING Hospital eventually offered Bill a position. It was a promotion where he would be in charge of a pre-hospital program for several counties. I liked the idea because it brought my friends closer to us. However, they had to leave their parents and Bill's boys in

Pittsburgh. Sometimes one has to go, but a father? Anyway, he accepted the job.

Bill and Mary started raising dogs. Chauncey sired Simon, but they needed a female, so they bought Pearl. Now they had three Springers in the house. Yes, they sprang all over me!

Then, Edie and I visited them during the winter.

"Look at the snow!" she exclaimed on our way there. "It's higher than our car!"

"That's just where the snow-plows made piles. We can make it."

The going was rough, but I was determined–foolish is a better word. We slipped and slid through the snow in our Chevette. My fingers felt like they were glued to the steering wheel.

"Look, we made it," I said as I finally parked in front of Bill and Mary's house.

"Just barely. We're lucky to be alive."

"You're exaggerating."

"I am?"

We met Bill and Mary at the door. As soon as we entered, Edie started to sneeze.

"It's the dogs," she said. "I'm allergic to 'em."

Edie never came again.

"Why don't you come down and lecture?" Bill asked me. "If we have time, we can play golf or poker and watch some movies."

With my experiences in the ER, lectures were easy for me. I liked public speaking anyway. To be introduced as an expert made me feel important.

However, the real reason I went to their house was the after-hours activities. We always made time for them. Pretty soon, I was going there twice a year for mini-vacations by myself in the spring and fall. We critiqued each other's writing–mostly mine–late at night over a glass of wine.

Often, Bill invited me to nearby golf courses. The match was mostly for bragging rights, but we both craved the competition. One day, the game was close. Bill had won the seventeenth hole to make it even. That meant Bill would drive first on the eighteenth[1]. If he drove well, then the pressure would be on me. The last hole was a par three over water. Bill examined it and even let a blade of grass go to determine the direction and intensity of the wind. He chose a five-iron and said, "Watch a pro do this."

Bill wiggled his club, then his body, and swung. His first shot went directly into the lake. Kerplunk!

Let's see. I give him a shot a hole. With the stroke and the penalty, that's two strokes. Now he's giving me a stroke. I like those odds.

Determined, Bill teed up another ball. The wiggle came next. That went right in, too. Kerplunk!

Now he's giving me three strokes. I can play safe and get a four. He'd have to get a hole-in-one in to tie.

Finally, he hit a beautiful shot that headed straight for the pin.

Uh-oh. He may just do that.

From the other end of the lake, a duck took wing. The bird flew towards the middle of the lake. The ball hit the duck in flight. The bird continued, but the ball plunged into the water below. Kerplunk!

The duck flew away. Red-faced, Bill didn't try to hit the fourth ball.

"You win the hole and the match," he angrily told me, then walked off the tee. Did you ever try to swing while you're laughing?

"WANTNA GO to a Risk Management meeting on Saturday evening?" Bill asked in one phone call.

"A what?"

"A Risk Management meeting."

"Just what I want to do with my Saturday."

"Are you off this weekend?"

"Why, yes."

"Then come on down. Sunday, we'll have all day."

"If anyone else was calling, I'd say 'No!' But because it's you, I'll be there." I answered reluctantly, thinking, *Who meets on Saturday evening?*

However, I drove there expecting a boring meeting. It was anything but that! The meeting was a poker game! In a way, it was 'Risk Management' because the big-wigs of the hospital played, as well as the minister. Where else could we get them all together?

Bill played in his poker hat, a white fedora with cards on it. I couldn't look at him without laughing.

We played all kinds of games, according to whoever dealt. It wasn't really poker, but it was fun.

We played until the wee hours of the morning. Mary had long since gone to bed.

SHE AND BILL were married in 1985. They were unable to have any children. So, they adopted two brothers, Jason and James. Odd, the older boy was called Jason. Now, Bill had two sons with that name. It was confusing.

The new boys were about seven and six.

"All our names begin with 'J,'" I said. "We should form a club."

"What will we call it?" James asked.

"That's easy, stupid," Jason snorted. "We'll call it the 'J' club."

"And Jason will be president. You, James, will be vice president."

"What will you be?" James asked.

"That's easy. You need someone to record the meetings, so I'll be the secretary."

"Isn't that a girl?" James asked.

"Sometimes it's a boy."

"We need a greeting," I said. "Something to start the meetings."

"How about an awesome handshake like this?" Jason did a little dance, tickled the palm of my hand, then grasped my wrist.

"Everybody has a handshake. Ours has to be special." I thought for a moment, then said, "I know. Get on the floor and form a circle."

"What are you doing?" James wondered as he got down.

"Now, remove your shoes and shake the foot of the person next to you with your foot."

The boys did it with each other, then with me. Thus, the foot shake was born.

I TRAVELED past a Carvel ice cream store to get to their house. I concocted a story. "I saw a sign in the window on the way down. It said, 'We made too much ice cream. Help us eat it.'"

"Can we go, Dad?" James asked, jumping up and down.

"Not only can we go, but we also have to help," Bill answered.

We drove to the ice cream store, where the boys ate ice cream like it was their first time.

AT ANOTHER TIME, Bill and I went hiking to prepare for one of our mountain climbs (more on them later). The night before, I asked Mary, "Do you have some Scotch Tape?"

"Of course. Doesn't everybody? Why?"

"Can I borrow it for tomorrow?"

"Aren't you taking the boys on a hike tomorrow?"

"Yes. And now we need some lollipops."

"Lollipops? We don't have any lollipops. We don't want the boys to get sugar too often. Ruins their teeth, and they don't sleep. What are you up to?"

"C'mon," I said to Bill. "We have to buy some."

Mary looked at us skeptically as Bill and I left for the lollipops.

"Maybe you two should lighten up. They're kids. Maybe you should watch *Mary Poppins*."

"Mary, who?"

I hit my forehead with my hand and shook my head as we drove to the store for lollipops.

In the morning, we went on what we considered an easy hike. We took the boys along. It was a way to bond. To secure their approval later, I taped lollipops to a tree out of view and off the trail. Before they saw what I'd done, I returned to them hiking with Bill. However, what is easy for an adult is not necessarily easy for a child.

"Why are you taking us on this stupid hike?" Jason complained as we walked up the mountain (We called it a mountain, but it was really a wooded hill, bald at the crest.)

"Are we near the top? Can we turn around yet?" James asked. Whining takes a lot of energy and air. It's a wonder they could breathe or didn't take off like a hot air balloon.

Finally, we reached the summit and were awed by the view.

On the way down, Bill whispered to me, "Maybe they want some cheese with their whine."

I stopped abruptly. "Shh! Did you hear that squirrel?"

Both boys shook their heads.

"He says there's a lollipop tree up ahead."

"What's a lollipop tree?" James asked.

"That's easy, stupid," Jason answered. "It's a tree that grows lollipops. Don't ya' know nothin'?"

James must have sprouted wings as he flew down the mountain, looking every which way for a lollipop tree. Jason hurried behind. We sat on a rock and watched as they searched. Suddenly, they stopped. The cellophane covering the candy glistened in the sunlight.

"I see it! I see it!" they shouted as they jumped up and down.

They headed for what looked like to the untrained eye, an ordinary maple tree. Dangling from its limbs were dozens of plastic-wrapped lollipops! They quickly forgot to whine as they ran for the candy. Their fatigue had been a state of mind. Thankfully, in their excitement, the boys didn't notice the tape. Jason and James started to tear the pieces of candy off the tree in delight.

"We have to bury one," I said, catching up to them.

Neither boy asked questions. In the ground, it went.

That childlike humility and faith are magnificent[2] .

When we finished, we returned to their house. The boys finally settled down and went to sleep. Like so many other nights, Bill and I watched a movie. Mary said demurely, "I prefer to read." At any rate, she left us alone for some male bonding.

We watched a Spike Lee[3] flick.

"*Do The Right Thing*. What a name for a movie! Does it mean that rioting is the right thing?" Bill asked after we watched the flick.

"I hope not. At least it's a better movie than *Eraserhead*."

"My home video is better than *Eraserhead*."

Bill and I often debated the state of the world. We argued from every viewpoint, both as changeable as the ocean.

In retrospect, I should have looked for the First Principle more. I could have discussed it with Bill. We were both lost and didn't know it. Bill and I were looking for lollipop trees and talking squirrels. It's far better to stick to GOD.

34

THE HIGHLAND AVENUE HOUSE

J osh and Jeremiah played soccer. Jim Dandy's[1] hired Jimmy as a cook He had lost his license and frequently depended on us for rides to and from work, although he had his own place. Shannon eventually played softball. Edie and I were always driving someone somewhere. Time was valuable.

I took the children bowling every week and played golf with Jimmy, Josh, and Jeremiah when it was warm. Louis Kreuger from across the street came whenever Jimmy couldn't, so we always had a foursome. Shannon was still too young.

"Computers are fun," Josh said to me one afternoon. "Why don't we get one?"

"Just what you need, another toy."

"They can improve your mind."

Kids know how to manipulate their parents. That was all I needed to hear, and I became convinced that computers were the way to go.

I thought the kids needed some moral teaching. I, unfortunately, excluded Christian principles as being outdated. So, what did I choose? I tried an even older system of belief – the Greeks. I didn't see the apparent contradictions.

"Tonight, we will start reading Aristotle's *Ethics*," I said one night to Josh. He rolled his eyes.

But you can't remove the legs from a table and expect it to stand.

"I hate this stuff," he said.

If I continued, Josh would start hating me. So, to our shame, we didn't raise them in any faith. Judeo-Christian morality is the best. What was I thinking?

Neither Edie nor I knew what we were doing, but between us were responsible for four children. We were experimenting. Try explaining that to a nine-year-old. We thought they needed something secure while growing up—an identity. Maybe the truth is more important.

Edie and I attended a meeting of mixed marriages, endeavoring to get guidance. A marriage between a Catholic and a Jew was considered a mixed marriage. But marriages are made in Heaven. Even though we were never legally wed and didn't have a piece of paper, we were still married.

Edie and I attended several meetings and discussed many problems. We discovered the other couples were looking to us for answers. At the time, I wasn't aware that we had any. We raised the kids to believe in humanity—a big mistake. I thought you tried to respond to situations by doing what was right. I should've asked, "Why?"

During that time, we continued to live at Welsh Hill Road. After three years, I finally completed the work on the rugs and walls.

"We should move," Edie said.

"But I just finished."

"That's the point. The house looks good"

So, we moved. The new house was still in Clarks Summit but on a steep hill on Highland Avenue in another section of town. The kids stayed at the same schools.

The big home had two stories. There were five bedrooms and a huge foyer/closet on the backside of a central fireplace. A pool, with two redwood sheds for changing and storage, was in the back. Inside the fence, behind the pool, was an elevated, flat lawn. You had to go up some steps to get there. I tried to grow a garden, but it was useless. The children converted it into a wiffleball field.

Outside the redwood fence was a hill that I had to mow. Who invented lawns, anyway?

"I don't like the plywood walls in the living room beside the brick wall," Edie said at one dinner.

Here we go. Against my better judgment, I asked, "Why?"

"Too dark."

So, I asked Bob Eckert, a friend from work, about it. "No problem. I can wallpaper them."

The dining area was connected to the living room, so that would need to be wallpapered, too.

After three layers of under-paper, Edie said, "I can still see the seam," by now, she was an expert at seeing them.

"I don't understand why it's showing," I said.

"But it is."

We gave up and hung the good gray marble paper atop it. The border was mauve and distracted one from the seam.

"What about the carpet?" Edie asked.

Know what that means.

"What do you suggest?"

"We should go shopping for a new carpet. The living room should be carpeted, but the dining room should be slate."

"You should be an interior decorator," I said sarcastically.

Edie ignored the remark.

The next day, we bought a wall-to-wall blue carpet with a divider for the living room. For the dining room, Edie and I purchased black slate.

"How do we clean it?" I asked.

"The salesman said to add vinegar to the water."

That was a royal pain in the butt. Oh, the sacrifices and rules we bend to save time or make something look good.

The wood holder for the corner fireplace was on the slate that divided the two rooms.

Edie pointed through a doorway to the other side of the fireplace "This is perfect for our rock collection." The chimney, which went through the middle of the house, had a back side. In it was a large foyer across from a big closet. Next to the chimney were built-in shelves where we put the kids' trophies. Below the shelves was a ledge where we could put our rock collection.

So, we put a rock in there that Johnny had given us.

"It comes from the Great Wall of China," he said.

We looked at him skeptically.

"It really does," he swore.

The rock was orange and very distinctive. We could not know if it came from the Great Wall. Seeing it, my father quipped, "Johnny probably got it in our backyard." On the other hand, knowing Johnny, he probably had smuggled it out of China.

A professor friend of Edie's ate dinner with us one night. During the meal, she handed me a little piece of concrete.

"What's this?" I asked.

"I happened to be in Berlin when the wall came down. That's a piece of it."

How do I know she's telling the truth? On the other hand, it is a good story.

Eventually, we put it alongside the one from the Great Wall of China. Now, how many people do you know that have rocks from both walls?

∾

WHEN THE TUB UPSTAIRS BROKE, "I think we should get a new one," Edie said.

I ordered a modular one-piece tub with a shower and fiberglass walls.

"How do we get it upstairs?" I wondered.

"We carry it."

"What do you mean 'we?'"

Getting it upstairs was a nightmare. Bob Eckert helped me. I couldn't have done it without his expertise.

On another occasion, Edie said of the kitchen, "I don't like this counter."

"Why?"

"Because it has these whorls in it that trap dirt."

"We can't replace it."

She pouted.

"Well, we can't. It's custom-made."

Edie finally relented.

During that time, we gradually transformed our library as we collected leather books to replace my paperbacks. Everywhere you looked, you found volumes. Our house looked like my parent's house, with books all over.

Someday, I'll be an author. Now, I'm somebody.

I puffed out my chest. Who was I kidding?

ONCE, after I had worked the three to eleven shift, I came home around midnight to find many young men sleeping on the living room floor. I woke them up. "Who are you?"

They didn't understand. I repeated, "Who are you?"

"*No Habla Ingles.*"

After my years with UFW I could read a little Spanish but did not understand when it was spoken. Edie came into the living room from upstairs to explain.

"They escaped from El Salvador. All of them dodged the draft there. If they get caught, a firing squad waits for them."

"What about my license? If I get caught, I will lose it and go to jail! And they're sleeping on my floor!"

What could I do? In effect, we were part of an Underground Railroad. The draft dodgers were *en route* to Canada. With my background, I had to let them stay. The next day, they disappeared, and I never saw them again. I didn't even know how many there were. Perhaps it's better that way.

EDIE AND I CELEBRATED EVERYTHING. You name it; we celebrated it. Because she is 100% Jewish, Edie didn't know how to make merry on Christmas. "I gave gifts to the bank teller and gas station attendant."

"What?"

"Wasn't I supposed to?"

"Actually, that's a good idea," I laughed.

I remembered why I had fallen in love with her. Beneath her sophisticated exterior, I think Edie might be a closet Christian.

One winter holiday, Edie and I were sitting in our dining room. Hanukkah usually comes at about the same time as Christmas, so we put up the tree and placed a menorah on the table. On the wall, facing the table, was a picture of a woman celebrating the Festival of Lights[2]. Johnny came from Japan with Yoko, his wife, and they spoke Japanese. Lena, married to Nick from Crete, were there, and they conversed together in Greek. To complete the scene, Dominic was visiting with Aracely, his wife. She was from Cuba. They chatted in Spanish.

The doorbell rang.

"Who's there?" I asked.

"The exterminator."

To get to the basement, we had to go through the dining room, where all the different languages were being spoken. The lit Christmas tree and menorah provided an unusual background.

As we descended to the basement, the exterminator nudged me, "What kind of a house is this, anyway?"

Good question. Lived here for ten years, and I still don't know.

35

THE KIDS

I never knew what to expect from any of our children. It was like living in a three-ring circus.

The first day Josh had his license, he came to me. "Dad, I've got something to tell you."

Uh-oh. This can't be good.

I put down the newspaper and said, "Go ahead. I'm listening"

"Hit a car today."

Ouch!

"Was anybody hurt?

"No."

At least I'm glad about that.

"Is the car okay?"

"Think so. Just needs a buff job. Except for the dent in the fender."

"What dent?"

"Oh, it's nothing. Just a little dent."

I looked at him skeptically.

The next day, the phone rang.

Who is it now?

"Hello?" I answered.

"This is Mr. Wright, the insurance adjustor on Joshua Thek's car."

Why is the insurance involved on a little fender-bender?

"And?" I asked, becoming nervous.

"We've decided to total it."

"What?" I exclaimed. "I thought it was a little dent."

He laughed into the receiver. "I don't know who told you that. But I wouldn't call the whole front end a 'little dent.'"

Kids often don't tell the whole truth.

I remembered how I had blown up a perfectly good engine as a teenager. I hung up a little wiser.

On another afternoon, we received a phone call. "This is the principal at Josh's school."

"What happened?" I exclaimed.

"Josh had a fistfight in the parking lot after school. He and the other boy are okay. But I will have to give them both detentions."

When he finally came home, I said, "Sit down."

And he took a seat across from me.

"Heard you got in a fight at school today," I began. "What was it about?"

"Nothing."

"Nothing! People don't hit each other for 'nothing.'"

"Nothing I can't handle."

Josh got up to leave. I put my hand on his shoulder and said, "Sit back down. You're not going anywhere until you tell me what happened."

We became stubbornly silent. I fixed my gaze on him.

"Well?" I said. "We can sit here all night if we have to."

And we sat silently for about an hour. It was very uncomfortable. It was like having ants crawl up your legs and unable to stop them.

Finally, when he understood how serious I was, he said, "Don't tell Mom. She'd have a cow."

I motioned with my right hand across my lips, indicating they were locked and sealed. After all, I was used to carrying secrets around at work. To be a doctor, you have to hold secrets. You won't be a doctor long if you blab all over town. The priest used to keep the secrets. Now it's the doctor.

"He was bullying me. Calling me names."

"Names? Like what?"

"Promise that you won't tell Mom."

"Promise."

"He called me 'Jew boy.'"

That information floored me.

Josh continued, "You always taught me to fight for what is right. Well, I did."

"There are other ways to fight without using violence."

Josh snorted. "Should I have asked him, 'Pretty please, don't call me that'? I'm sure he would've stopped."

I was losing the argument big time, and I knew it.

"Maybe we should tell the principal."

"I wouldn't do that."

"Why?"

"Because the bully is the principal's son."

I felt trapped.

Hate to admit it, but he's right. Time to turn the other cheek.

"You can go now," I said, secretly proud of his stance. I went upstairs to our bedroom, where Edie was half-asleep. Any thought that I would get a reprieve quickly vanished.

"Well?" she asked.

"That's a deep subject."

"Very funny. What did the boys fight about?"

"Kid's stuff."

"That doesn't sound like my Josh."

"But it sounds a lot like *my* Josh!" I retorted, hoping to divert her attention.

Edie opened her mouth, thought better of it, and shut it again, becoming quiet.

That wasn't so bad.

I undressed, got into bed, and turned out the light.

THEN THERE WAS JEREMIAH. Although he would never refer to himself this way, he was a typical middle child. Josh was the oldest, Shannon the youngest, and Jimmy was already gone. So, Jeremiah drew attention to himself through athletics. First, it was soccer. Then it became bodybuilding. There was a contest of "Mister Pennsylvania Without Steroids," which he entered and eventually won. My "little" boy had muscles on muscles and was not so "little" anymore.

Before becoming "Mr. Pennsylvania," he had become notorious for being the detention king of Clarks Summit. He already had a reputation by eighth grade. One afternoon the phone rang again.

"This is the principal at Jeremiah's school."

By now, I was used to the calls.

"What did he do now?"

"It seems his friend put a lit cigarette in the wastebasket and left. Jeremiah left, too. The garbage caught fire. The sprinklers were activated. Fire engines arrived. We evacuated the school. Jeremiah won't say who did it."

Good for him!

"What's the penalty if he doesn't tell? I asked.

"Suspension and Community Service."

Jeremiah, to his credit, didn't squeal.

However, after that, I feared going to the mailbox because a letter from the school was sure to be inside.

One Sunday, we were eating out with my parents when Dad turned to fourteen-year-old Jeremiah and asked, "Do you know the German for A-bomb?"

Jeremiah shook his head.

Dad just invented words and made them sound German by stringing them together by adding "en"s.

"Loudenboomen."

I almost choked on my drink.

Better ignore it. It will never come up again in conversation.

After a few minutes, Dad again turned to Jeremiah, "Do you know the German for H- bomb?"

Again, Jeremiah shook his head.

"Loudenboomen *mitt* blows hole in grounden."

Again, I was stunned. Adding the *mitt* was an act of genius and added authenticity to Dad's whole explanation.

How do I tell Jeremiah that his grandfather is pulling his leg?

Edie looked at me, but I averted her gaze.

However, Jeremiah didn't take long to use that supposed knowledge. The very next day, he asked his German teacher in class, "What is the German word for A-bomb?"

"There isn't one."

"Yes, there is."

"Well, I don't know it."

"It's 'loudenboomen.'"

He received detention. It was good that Jeremiah didn't ask for the German word for H-bomb.

AND, there was our baby, Shannon, I don't know how she survived growing up with three older brothers.

One night, Shannon, who was four or five at the time, couldn't sleep. She rose from bed and stood on the stairs leading to the family room below where I watched T.V. I could see her legs first, but the ceiling hid her face. Shannon hadn't descended the stairs far enough yet. I could see her tiny legs dancing on the stairs. Our eyes met when she came down the stairs farther, and she stopped. I saw, by her face, she was searching for an excuse for being out of bed.

"And what are you doing up, young lady?"

"I had a nightmare."

"Do you want to tell me about it?"

"No."

"Why not?"

"Because it's PG13."

The very next night, Shannon's legs danced on the stairs again. She met my stare and halted.

"What are you doing now, young lady?"

"I had another nightmare."

Against my better judgment, I proceeded, "Do you want to tell me about it?"

"I'm pregnant."

"What!"

"And I'm gonna name him Freddie."

I was being paid back with interest. Now, I ask you, how can anyone stay angry at answers like those? I surrendered and laughed.

Shannon was fond of talking (Does that sound familiar?). She was around six when one day the phone rang in our kitchen. I was in the dining room speaking with Dad, who was visiting, so Shannon answered. After a long twenty minutes, she hung up and joined us.

"Who was it?" I asked.

"Don't worry about it."

"Why?"

"It was a wrong number."

Another time, eight-year-old Shannon was having trouble with her homework and faced me. She put out her right hand and commented, "This is west, right?"

I nodded my head.

Shannon turned around. She stuck out her right hand again. "This is west, right?" Shannon had a problem with directions.

36

COUSIN LENA

Cousin Lena had married Nick from Crete. It was partly a marriage of convenience because Nick wanted to stay out of the draft. It didn't work. Nick got drafted by both the Greek Navy and the American Army. I don't know how he did it, but he avoided both. Maybe the two kids kept him out. I'll never know. Anyway, what started as a marriage of convenience was transformed into a real marriage.

They had been living in Alaska because of one of his hare-brained schemes to make money. But he hadn't figured on all the ice and snow. When he heard that I had been working as a doctor, they showed up in Pennsylvania.

Nick was a short-order cook. Lena and he wanted their own business. I offered them the money, had the location chosen, and the owner of The Waffle House even signed the papers. Then, Nick reneged: the deal, and Lena's marriage disintegrated. He departed, or so I thought. Now my cousin and her two children were homeless.

"What am I gonna do?" Lena wondered.

"Simple. You and the kids will move in with us."

"That's good of you, but how? I know this house is big, but not that big."

"We'll have to make it bigger," Edie said. "We'll add on."

"Yeah. Mike and Josh can share a room," I said. "They'll be like brothers. You and Kathryn will have your own rooms. What is family for?"

"Where are you and Edie gonna sleep?"

"Don't worry. We'll find a way," I replied, trying to sound confident. The truth was I had no idea how we would do it.

I called the tax office. They set over a Mr. Smiley, a bureaucrat with a colossal briefcase. "Let's see," he began rubbing his chin. Dollar signs appeared in his beady, brown eyes as he considered the possibilities with glee. "If you expand the house horizontally the taxes will go up accordingly."

"That's out," I replied. "Don't want to give Uncle Sam more than I need to."

With that, Mr. Smiley closed up his scrolls and put them hurriedly back into his briefcase. He left, acting as if he was personally offended.

I looked at Edie and said, "What did I say?"

"You said you don't want to line his pocket."

"I did?"

That night, I dreamed about it. Some people would say that GOD spoke to me. In the dream, I saw the house going up, not out.

"I've got it!" I screamed, sitting up straight in bed.

"What is it you got?" the half-asleep Edie said groggily.

"Mr. Smiley said our tax base would increase if we add on horizontally. He didn't say anything about vertically."

And that's what we did. So, it would be up and not out.

I had a crane remove the roof. It hovered in the air attached to the crane while the walls went up, and we had added a new story. My office, a studio, a full bath, and a master bedroom replaced the attic. There were skylight windows and a pole to open them. It was like having our own, private apartment.

Lena and Edie became good friends. My cousin had her own bedroom on the first floor. Everything in it—the paneling, the carpet, the phone—was blue. We christened it the "Blue Room." Jeremiah's room was next to hers. By then, Jimmy had his own place.

Mike shared the big bedroom that used to be mine and Edie's on the second floor with Josh. Shannon slept in the one next to them. Kathryn had her own near the top of the stairs beside the laundry cubicle. She had a congenital defect that would approach blindness as Kathryn grew and went through puberty. Everyone was protective of her.

We enrolled the kids in school. I was busy taking the boys to sporting activities. Josh and Mike loved baseball and collected cards.

"Want to go to the flea market again this weekend to get some cards?" I asked each week.

"Sure," they always said.

And that's what we did almost every Saturday. Our collection blossomed.

There were cards, cards, and more cards. I had a collection of my own that I had as a kid. In today's world, it would be worth a ton of money. But we inadvertently threw it away.

That's not gonna happen again.

Then, Nick returned.

"I'll divorce him," a determined Lena claimed.

Then, he stalked the house. I never knew when Nick was going to appear.

"This is not fair to you guys," a frightened Lena protested.

"Come on," the sneakered Edie said, "We'll get a restraining order on him. Nobody's gonna scare *me* in my own house!"

Nick and Lena tried a temporary separation. I thought that was the first step to a divorce and that it was over between them. However, Nick was adamant. After all, he was the father of two children. Nick stuck to it and, eventually, won the battle. In the end, Lena and the children moved back with him. I'm not sure why Lena went back. Perhaps, she didn't want to involve us in her mess any longer. Maybe she felt more secure with him. Possibly, in a weird way, she did love him. I don't know.

They moved into an apartment complex a couple of miles from us. Things seemed to be working smoothly. But then, the wheels came off,

One evening, I received a frantic phone call from Kathryn.

"He's got a gun!" she screamed into the phone.

"Calm down. Calm down. Who's got a gun?"

"My father! He's pointing it at my mother! Can you come over right now?"

"Whoa. Me? What am I gonna do? Sounds like a time for the police."

"The police will only spook him! I dunno what you'll do! Maybe talk to him? Please, Uncle Joe?"

So, I prepared to leave. I never thought that he might use the gun on me. I probably wouldn't have gone if I had thought of the possibilities. GOD protects the stupid.

"Where's my coat?" I asked Edie.

"In the closet. Why"

I found it and then put it on. Hurriedly, I went to the door.

"Where are you going?" Edie asked.

I didn't answer but just left the house. Getting in my Chevette, I was off. Breaking the speed limit, I raced over.

If he touches her, I'll–

I took a corner on two wheels.

If I get there!

Finally, I arrived at their apartment complex. After parking the car, I ran to where they lived. I pounded on the door.

Kathryn met me there. "Come in quick!" she whispered breathlessly. "He's in the kitchen."

So, I hurried to the kitchen. There, on the table was a pistol. I didn't know what kind. Does it matter? I knew they were dangerous, though I'd never fired one myself. At the other end of the table sat Nick.

I can make a move for it. No! He's closer. Probably waiting for me to do something stupid, then grab it. No! I have to gain his confidence. Have him give me the gun.

So, I pulled out a chair and then sat across from him. The gun was pointed in my direction. I gulped. The silence was deafening.

Now what? Can't stay in this stand-off. Have to say something. Defuse the situation.

I knew he had a brother in Canada who owned a restaurant.

"How is Jason doing?"

"All right," he said in his broken English.

"Just 'all right?'"

"Business good."

"How so?"

"He's making lot of money. I went up to help him couple months ago."

"You did?" I asked, even though I had heard the story before from Lena.

"Yeah. Got him started. Came back when business pick up."

Oh great! Left us holding the bag while you played the saint! Better not ruffle his feathers now, though.

"It's turning cold," I said. "Does it ever get cold in Crete?"

He smiled. "Sometimes. But not much. Even when it does, lasts few days. Crete is – how you say–"

Nick moved his arms in a circle. It was like playing Charades.

"The whole world?" I asked.

He shook his head. Then he moved his arms in a circle again.

"Everything?'

Again, he shook his head. He moved his arm in a circle a third time.

Come on. Think! What does he mean?

I looked again at the gun on the table and gulped.

Maybe it's around. Surround. I got it!

"The warm waters of the Mediterranean surround Crete?"

Nick nodded enthusiastically.

"You make good interpreter," he said,

"I do?"

"Taking my driver's test soon. Need interpreter."

"Lena speaks Greek. I don't. She would make a great interpreter."

"We argue about that."

"And?"

"Decided she no good interpreter. Need someone else. Someone like you."

"But I don't know any Greek."

"Do not need to."

"Whoa! An interpreter who can't speak the language?"

"I speak English. But can't read. Need you to read it for me."

I had to admit, but there was a logic to this madness. My eyes were drawn again involuntarily to the gun.

"Could think much clearer if that gun wasn't staring me in the face."

"Oh, that," Nick said. "It not even loaded." He picked it up and turned it around, pointing the nozzle at him and the handle toward me. "Here. Take it before it cause trouble."

And so, we defused the situation, and I became an interpreter.

Then they moved away to New Jersey, temporarily out of our lives, leaving us with a much bigger house.

37

DISNEY WORLD

Disney World was the Holy Grail of adventure parks. It was touted to be for the whole family, and, in many ways, it was. Who didn't want to go on the rides and see the exhibits and parades? It was like being a kid again. Everybody wanted to go to Disney World. I was no exception.

For weeks, I had planned the winter trip to Florida. I read books on what was a "must-see." I had everything figured out. The one thing I didn't take into account was—us.

I took my family there twice. The first time we stayed in a hotel room. I spent all my time making arrangements, but the best I could do was rent a single room.

"Does it have a TV?" Josh anxiously asked once we were inside the room.

"That's the only thing you have to say? I bust my butt getting here, and all you can ask is if there's a TV? Why?"

"I want to watch the Super Bowl," the pubescent Josh whined.

I reacted angrily. "We come to Florida, and you want to watch a stupid football game!"

"It's not just any game, Dad. This is the Super Bowl!"

I left the room, slamming the door behind me. I was miserable despite visiting the amusement parks. I couldn't get over the lack of gratitude. Our heavenly FATHER must feel the same way.

The second time was great! I had learned how not to do things the first time. Richard and Regina had a time-share in a two-storied condo they wanted to loan us. "

How do we use it?" Edie asked.

"Just watch," I replied. "If anyone asks, your name is Regina."

"Regina! Whoa! What cockamamie scheme do you have cooked up?"

I pulled into the resort and parked. Edie and I went to the front desk. A clerk with dyed blonde hair sat behind the counter, reading a book. I could see her black roots as she had her head buried in the book.

I rang the bell. Without raising her eyes, she continued reading.

"This is the good part where the guy gets the girl. I'll be with you in a minute."

I was outraged. I rang the bell loudly twice.

Finally, the clerk raised her eyes, squinted through her dyed-blonde hair that had tumbled across her eyes, and looked at me. "Where's the fire?"

"We have a condo that we want to occupy."

"Name?"

"Richard Thek." Edie poked me in the ribs. I ignored her.

"ID?"

I took my driver's license out and put it on the counter.

"Say, it says here your name is Joseph," the clerk said, eyeing me suspiciously.

"That's my legal name, but I go by Richard."

She looked again at the license. "I don't understand. This license says 'New Jersey.' But our records indicate you live in Delaware."

"Just moved. Haven't changed the license yet."

The clerk let out a snort. Wanting to return to her romance novel, she whispered to herself, "Don't pay me to think. If they did, I'd be a millionaire. It's no skin off my nose." She validated our papers, and we were in.

Edie said on the way back to the car, "That was quite a performance in there. Did you ever think what kind of an example you're setting for the kids?"

"All I know is we have the condo."

The condo was beautiful, with three bedrooms. Shannon slept on the pull-out couch.

Jen, Josh's girlfriend then, came along, so he was happy and out of our hair. I didn't see them all the time we were there. Chaperoning? What's that? Who chaperones the chaperones? I would never approve of that arrangement now, but then I thought differently.

I studied Disney World again and concluded, "We can see it all in three days."

"This isn't a contest." Edie tried to restore a little reason.

"For fifty dollars a day, it sure is!"

"Oh, brother!"

We spent one day each at EPCOT, MGM, and Fantasyland. I went with Edie, Jeremiah, and Shannon.

"Hurry up," I urged continually.

"Rome wasn't built in a day," Edie complained.

We rode almost all the rides—whirling around in the Tea Cups, being Captain Nemo in the Nautilus submarine, Thunder Mountain, Pirates of the Caribbean, and seeing how they made different movies. The songs rang in my head, "Yo, ho, ho, it's a pirate's life for me," and who could forget, "It's a small world after all!" But we skipped Space Mountain thinking that the kids were too young. Besides that, we saw everything—Tom Sawyer's cave, Cinderella's castle, the Haunted House with its holograms, The American Adventure, where Mark Twain and Ben Franklin seemed to come alive, and The Hall of the Presidents. Then there were the different countries and their pavilions. We hurried here and ran there. For MGM and Fantasyland, we finished in the afternoon, and for EPCOT, we ended in the evening. The four of us saw Illuminations[1] after eating dinner at the German pavilion. It had been a top-ten trip!

JOSH GRADUATED FROM HIGH SCHOOL, moved to Philadelphia, and became a student at Drexel University. Now the house was way too big. Jeremiah moved into the old master bedroom on the second floor, and Shannon kept hers.

38

WORK

Some of this is difficult to write about. My humor is often a defense against the blood, the gore, the decapitations, the knife and gunshot wounds. We must keep things in perspective and remember we were a city ER. Yes, we enjoyed our work, but we never let our fun divert us from providing good care. The patients came first. We were able to switch gears from laughing to being deadly serious at a moment's notice.

A good ER needs good administration. Peter Lynch and I tried to provide some of that. There is always something going on behind the scenes.

The first year at Mercy Hospital[1] I was finally making money. I thought I deserved it. After all, there had been four years of medical school followed by three years of a grueling residency.

At first, the administration assigned four doctors to the ER. I was in charge of the schedule. Peter Lynch, whose job was to oversee me, took care of everything else.

The ER was changing. It was no longer just for emergencies but was a clinic, too. Poor people, who couldn't get appointments with doctors, flooded the ER. This translated into our being busy most of the day and night. At one time, you could get some sleep while working the night shift or trade war stories during the day or evening. That was no longer true.

"ER is a specialty now," I said to Peter.

"Aren't all ER docs temporary?" he asked, parroting the administration's opinion.

"I hope not."

"Aren't they just waiting to open offices of their own? Why would anyone want the ER as a career?"

I looked at him askance because that was precisely how I'd been trained.

"Take a stiff like me, for instance," I said. "The ER is a good fit with normal shifts. I can be a good husband and father *and* be a doctor. I've seen enough of spending too much time on your work—failed marriages, troubled children. No thanks."

I tried to let that sink in before continuing. "And then there's the payment. I never have to worry about whether people can afford treatment. You guys take care of that. I can just take care of people. It's what I always wanted to do."

However, no matter what I said, I couldn't get him to understand or change his attitude.

ONE HUNDRED SIXTY-EIGHT HOURS A WEEK, split four ways, equals forty-two. It was too much. We tried twelve-hour shifts – four days on followed by three days off. It was a band-aid, something to kick the can down the road. Then Jim Harley, one of the doctors, left.

"Say, we need a fifth doctor," I recommended to Peter Lynch one day, taking advantage of the crisis.

"We do?"

"Yeah, we do. It would make life so much easier. We all would stay."

He didn't want to lose me, too, so he said, "I'll see what I can do."

Peter got it approved by Sister, and, as a result, I recruited Dominic and Phil Bocci. They had finished their residencies at Geisinger—Dom in Emergency Medicine and Phil in Internal

Medicine. I remembered Phil Bocci from moonlighting at Hazleton's St. Joe's.

We should hire anybody on time going up that mountain in a snowstorm.

Dominic was my friend. Of course, I would recommend him.

"They're rock-solid both as people and as doctors. I'd hire them before someone else does," I suggested to Peter Lynch.

"You're the expert," he said.

And, so, he did it.

Now we have two trained ER docs. I'm not alone anymore.

I became the Director as promised, but the hospital's ideas of a department were different from mine. I was in charge of the doctors but not the nurses.

I should tell them to "Get Lost." But I have a mortgage and a family with bills. Besides, there's no guarantee that any other place is better. You can train a dog you know better than one you don't. Things could be a lot worse.

I can't uproot my family again. It's not just me.

So, I decided to stay.

"You will eventually get your own department," Sister assured me many times. I never did.

The schedule included vacation time, personal days, and holidays. Every five weeks' rotation included one week off. It worked. There was plenty of time to rest and putter about the house. Or, you could take a mini-vacation.

Then, Jerry Carter, another of the original four, moved to Florida. I replaced him for twelve months with Scott Boone, a year behind Dom in Emergency Medicine.

Now, we have three ER-trained doctors. Wow! Things are looking up.

Mercy had a competition with Community Medical Center (CMC), another hospital in Scranton.

"We don't trust Mercy," Tim, one of the seasoned paramedics, said.

Don't blame him. I don't trust them, either.

The gist was that they had a Mobile Intensive Care Unit (MICU[2]) and Mercy wanted its own. I brought in a doctor from Pittsburgh to critique our facilities.

"We need someplace for the helicopter to land," Sister said after he had left.

"A heliport won't work. The buildings surrounding Mercy are too high," I explained, but I might as well advise a fish not to swim.

She had visions of grandeur, and I had switched to a different script that Sister didn't like.

"Don't want to die on the vine," she said.

Are you listening?

Mercy and CMC eventually reached a compromise. We'd become the Regional Resource Center, and they'd be the Regional Trauma Center with the heliport. Mercy owned its own MICU by then, but now CMC had two. I think it was like a toy to Sister. Whoever had the most would win. Life shouldn't be that way at all[3].

On our MICU, security drove, and we had a nurse on board. They replaced one of the two paramedics.

"We're losing jobs when nurses ride and security drives," Tim complained.

"Any solutions?"

"Yeah, get them off the MICUs."

"Ain't gonna happen. Sister wants them there."

ONE EARLY EVENING it was quiet until I received a call on the radio from the MICU. They were *en route* to our hospital.

"We have a twenty-something male involved in an MVA[4]. BP of 70. Can we apply the MAST[5] trousers? Over."

"Good idea. Over."

Moments later, the paramedics rolled him into a previously quiet ER. Blood was everywhere. The paramedics had applied the MAST trousers.

Probably saved his life.

Everything else stopped as we tried to prevent death. The stillness had changed in a matter of seconds. The medical personnel descended upon the unconscious patient like vultures on a dead carcass. But unlike vultures, they were hoping the young man pulled through. The charge nurse, Kay Schmidt, drew the curtain separating Trauma Bay One and Trauma Bay Two, so we had plenty of room to work.

"What happened?" I yelled above the din accompanying the event.

"Car against telephone pole," a paramedic explained. "Telephone pole won."

"Did he have on his seat belt?

"No."

I examined the patient quickly, paying particular attention to his chest.

"Looks like he broke a few ribs. Probably cut something. Who's on for CV[6] surgery?"

"Oh *#*#. It's Hammurabi," Kay muttered.

I was new, so I'd never met the illustrious Dr. Hammurabi.

"Call him."

In ten minutes, he arrived. He was a little man of Syrian heritage. It was hard to take him seriously as he wore his tennis outfit. But like so many doctors, he suffered from having a GOD complex.

"Get out of way!" he yelled as if only he could save the patient. He cowed us all into submission. Then Dr. Hammurabi started to tear off the MAST trousers.

"Whoa!" I shouted. "Leave them alone. They're saving his life!"

But he wouldn't listen. Dr. Hammurabi removed the MAST trousers.

We lost his blood pressure. That's when I finally took over.

"Nurse Schmidt, reapply the MAST!"

She did. But it was too late. The patient died.

If only I'd been more aggressive, I second-guessed myself.

Dr. Hammurabi said, "If only I called sooner, I could save patient."

I saw red. "You killed him!" I yelled. Starting to lunge for him, I would have wrung his tiny neck. Nurse Schmidt stepped between us.

"The two of you should go to separate corners."

"Especially him," Dr. Hammurabi said.

"Why you—"

With the help of a security guard whom she had called for help, Nurse Schmidt removed me from the area. Outside the pulled curtain, I cooled down. Dr. Hammurabi exited to the tennis court, leaving me to explain to the family that their loved one had died.

We had a separate grieving room. Telling people that their loved one has died is a class in medical school they don't have. They should. I guess they presume that we can save anyone. However, every death is not premature. But temporarily, we *can* prevent some. This was one of them, and I knew it. Like I said before, the very people we need to grieve with and for we cannot tell the whole truth because of the threat of a lawsuit. What a society!

One look at my face and the pregnant wife knew he had died.

"What are we gonna do?" she wailed.

I had no answer then. I just hugged her.

ON ANOTHER EVENING SHIFT, we received a radio call.

"We've got an elderly man who went down ..." and then only static because of interference from the mountains. Since it was a one-way radio, I had to wait until the paramedic finished. "... Can I give him a bolus of Epinephrine? Over."

"I didn't copy. Repeat. Over."

"An elderly man went down ..." nothing but static again. I waited until the static stopped.

"Where are you? Over."

Finally, I heard a voice say, "The Notch. Over."

"This is not working," I commented to Betty Anne Laguna, the nurse beside me. "The paramedics must be trained so they can act on their own."

But Betty Anne, the charge nurse that night, was worried about the rooms being full.

"Dr. Thek, where are we gonna put him?"

There was a man behind the curtain in Trauma Bay One who was okay. I had just ordered a chest x-ray to ensure he hadn't pneumonia.

"I know. Move the patient from Trauma One to the hallway."

Then, the radio blared.

"Got a cardiac arrest ..." Then more static.

"Oh, *#*#!" I exclaimed. "I can't hear what they're doing!"

She moved the patient from Trauma Room One into the hallway.

The cardiac arrest patient went in there when he arrived. We coded him for half an hour before declaring him dead.

However, we never changed the x-ray request due to the bustle. The suite where the tech took films was right behind the nurses' station. The technician on duty came down, took the dead body, and snapped a chest. I don't know how you can take a picture of a stiff, but she did. Then, the tech noticed he wasn't breathing and panicked. "Code! Code! He's not breathing!"

I ran into the room, not recognizing the cardiac arrest patient. The paramedics, who brought him, thought I had started a trend. First, you pump on the chest for a half-hour, stop, expose them to radiation, and begin again.

I called a code.

"Dr. Thek, this is the man from Trauma One," Betty Anne informed me as she pulled on my sleeve.

I pushed her away. "I don't care where he's from!" It had yet to register with me. I kept on pumping. Then, it dawned on me that I was coding the same man twice!

I called it off, but the patient developed a heart rhythm on the monitor when we stopped! Now, what was I going to do? I would have to code him a third time if the beat kept up.. The paramedics supposed I was a genius. Betty Anne thought I was a dunce. The rhythm stopped, and I didn't have to cross that bridge. The man was pronounced dead for a second time. To GOD it's only once[7]. But to man, it's twice. We have to learn the difference.

I HAD to do something about the static problem. We had the regular monthly medical meeting. I was nervous beforehand. However, there was a lot of opposition from, of all people, doctors.

Have to broach the subject of protocols for the paramedics on the MICU.

The chief of medicine, Dr. McAndrew, went through old business and asked, "Do we have anything new to discuss?"

I raised my hand sheepishly.

He recognized me. "Yes, Doctor Thek, the floor is yours."

I stood up and cleared my throat. Doctor McAndrew offered me a microphone.

"I don't think I'll need it," I said. "Can everyone hear me?"

The doctors in the back of the room nodded.

"Patients are not getting the medicine needed to save their lives because of radio interference. They are at risk. Who knows how many have already died because of static? Establishing protocols so paramedics don't have to get everything okayed by a doctor first would help save lives."

Dr. Hammurabi, the chest surgeon, stood up and, in his broken English, said, "I against it. Do not need cowboys running around playing doctor."

I became angry thinking of the dangerous situations that paramedics and first responders often faced.

"'Cowboys!' They go where no one else will. We should have some respect for them."

"Doctor wanna-be, all of them."

I turned red and wanted to deck him.

Dr. McAndrew intervened. "We'll see what Sister thinks about it."

I already knew that she wanted her own MICU. And we wouldn't get a MICU without protocols. I smiled smugly and regained my seat. There were no more objections, and the measure eventually passed.

We developed criteria. Rather than letting patients die, protocols were initiated through the local EMS[8].

I HELD a meeting concerning retirement at my house. I wanted to be sure everyone was covered. To do that, all of us would have to join forces.

"I have to act independently on this," Charley Sheer, the lone original left, informed us.

"That will destroy the group," I countered.

"That's unfortunate."

That night, I tossed and turned in bed. I couldn't get to sleep and kept looking at the clock.

3:45. Only five minutes. Can't be.

I pulled up the cover and turned again. After a while, I was still awake. I turned back and snuck a peek at the clock.

3:50! Is there something wrong with the clock?

Finally, I realized, *This is ridiculous! I have to fire him if the department is to move forward. But he's been here longer than me. I respect him. But it has to be done. Oh, why can't someone else be in charge? I just want to care for people.*

A couple of days later, when we were alone in a car, I thought this was the right opportunity. "Charley, you're holding us back," I began.

"How?"

Just be honest, a little voice inside me prompted.

I took a deep breath. "You know we can't form a group without your agreement, so I must let you go."

"What!"

"I tried to explain the other night."

Charley started to hyperventilate.

"Just calm down," I soothed.

"That's easy for you to say! I have bills!"

I wanted to say *you should have thought of them the other night.*

After a pregnant pause, he continued calmly, "When is my last day?"

"Two weeks."

"To tell you the truth, I knew I had to get out. I'm getting older. I need to start my own practice. This provides the impetus."

"We can help."

"Thanks."

With that, we parted friends.

I hope I never have to fire anyone again. But I did.

DOM AND PHIL opened up their own practice together—fulfilling Peter Lynch's prophecy. Each doctor went part-time in the ER, sharing one full-time position. Where there were two before, now there was one. Scott Boone moved to Florida, so he and Charley had to be replaced.

"We need double coverage," I informed Peter Lynch. "The census keeps increasing."

"I'll see what I can do."

Mercy was on the rising part of the bell curve. So, I recruited four ER-trained docs. I knew them from Geisinger. Now, we were seven doctors, six ER trained, probably the only place in the country with that many.

39

DAY SHIFT

We worked three shifts: days, evenings, and nights. Double coverage was only three days a week and only for doctors. Each shift had its own personality. Days were mainly career nurses, evenings were single nurses, and nights were not as busy. Besides that, you could work nights and raise a family.

I grew to know everyone there—doctors, nurses, maintenance people, security guards, social workers, cafeteria workers—everybody. The ER was the hub. You never knew who you might need for a favor or to whom you could provide one. Take, for instance, Obstetrics. At first, the obstetrician wasn't in the hospital on evenings or nights, so I got used to delivering babies—maybe one hundred. But they were there when I needed them. One hand washed the other.

I ran to cardiac arrests, or codes as we called them. We could run a code. Regular GPs[1] often didn't want to despite knowing the patient. I suspect their reluctance was because they didn't know how to.

When a patient was declared dead, without fail, the nursing supervisor, Ann Marie Rowlette, opened a window. She was tall for a lady, about 5'10", and always intimidating.

What's she doing that for?

My wonder increased to curiosity.

Finally, one night, I had had enough. Despite her demeanor, I asked stupidly, "Why are you doing that?"

Ann Marie scowled at me as if I was an idiot. Looking at me askance, she replied, "Why, to let the spirit out."

The nursing supervisor said it so that it inferred that everyone knew that.

THE DAY SHIFT was usually busy—too busy for my liking. I tried to switch to as many nights as I could. Being the director in control of the schedule had its advantages. But I had to work some days; after all, I was the director. However, the nights away from home strained our marriage. After all, I had my own family and Lena's to be concerned about. I tried to juggle both worlds as best I could—sometimes successfully, sometimes not.

The nurses were always talking about something—anything to keep their minds off work. It could be movies, restaurants, news—whatever. Once, in the newspaper, atheists were complaining about school prayer and Christmas songs.

"How can anyone not believe?" Michelle Abington, one of the nurses, wondered out loud.

How could anyone believe? I naively questioned at the time. I had yet to undergo my metamorphosis. I was still in the larval stage cocoon. Looking back, I wonder how I could be so dense, especially delivering a baby with those little parts all working. Some people, like me, said there were no miracles. Perhaps we're not looking and miss them.

During a rare slow day, one of our nurses got pulled to work the floor. As we sat around the conference room table, I said, "Look at our nurses being pulled from the ER when it's not busy. Everybody suffers. It makes more sense if ER nurses report directly to me. We don't need the nursing supervisors, many of whom have never worked in the ER."

You would have thought that I dropped a bomb in the room. Nobody said a word. Then Ann Marie Rowlette came in and sat.

Now the nurses will never talk with her here. Don't I have support from any of them?

"We'll stay put under nursing," Joan Kraft, the head nurse, said, finally breaking the difficult silence. "They're dependable." That brought a rare smile to Ann Marie's face.

I guess Joan thinks I'm not. With the history here, I'm not surprised. Better shut up for now.

And I did, for once.

But their future was in the hospital, not me.

Joan left for a teaching job in the hospital, and Jackie Splawn became the new head nurse.

Good things come to those who wait.

I thought things would change, but they didn't – at least, not to my liking. The ER was still part of Family Practice, not a separate entity. The RNs were still part of the Nursing Department led by Anne Marie Rowlette.

Ann Marie should check her brain waves to make sure she's not flat line.

People brought us a hot meal down from the cafeteria. I ate my lunch quickly on days. Most times I sat at the conference room table across from the nurse's station. It had a window through which I could see if they were busy or not. I often had my meal interrupted because a patient needed immediate attention. By the time I returned, the food was cold.

One afternoon, after having my lunch interrupted by a patient who had slit her wrists, I returned and my food was cold.

"I'm sick of this!" I complained.

Jackie Splawn sat across from me. "Can't do anything about it," she said.

"Yes, we can! We can get a microwave!"

"Good idea! Have to run it by Jean Marie."

Oh, great! I'm sure she'll come up with some reason why we can't.

And, later that day, Jackie presented the idea to Ann Marie. "No!" she said emphatically. "Too expensive."

That ended it. Ann Marie had spoken.

The next day, I was still fuming. You could've fried an egg on my head. Anyway, I waited for the conference room to be empty. Making sure that no one saw me, I entered it. Closing the curtains on the window, I took a red marker and printed the word "UNION" in big, red letters on the white blackboard. Then I slipped out of the room. Jackie Splawn was at the nurse's station and saw me leave. I picked up some charts and got busy with a few patients pretending everything was fine. In about five minutes, I heard a scream. I went to the nurse's station. A nurse emerged from the conference room to whisper something in Jackie Splawn's ear. With that, Jackie gets on the telephone. Almost immediately, Anne Marie Rowlette comes thundering into the ER.

"Who did it? Who did it?"

She entered the conference room and left the door open so everyone could see her. Ann Marie quickly erased the blackboard.

When she came out, she was quaking. Her face was red and she looked like she was going to explode. She looked directly at me.

"Who did this?"

There was mute silence after her question.

"Did anyone see who did this?"

I readied myself for something from Jackie Splawn. There was still silence.

Jean Marie left and I breathed a sigh of relief, but she knew I was responsible.

A few days later, I was eating my lunch across from Jackie Splawn in the conference room. She says, "Maybe we should request a microwave again."

I shook my head. "Jean Marie will only shoot it down."

"What if we don't involve her?"

"Now how will we do that? She is the head of nursing you know."

"It's all in the presentation."

"What do you mean?"

"If it involves medical care, isn't that the doctors' ballpark?"

"Now, how do we have getting a microwave be medical care?"

"Simple. Just say the patients might need heated blankets. Who can object to that if the nurses use it to warm their food?"

I looked at her and squinted while scratching my chin. "That just might work"

"Oh, one thing. Just say it was your idea. I'd be fired if Jean Marie catches wind that it was mine."

Jackie got up to leave.

Probably had it all planned. I've been had, but who cares?

I presented it at the next medical meeting. And it was approved. We had a microwave. I realized that Jean Marie had become my enemy while Jackie Splawn had become my friend.

Not bad. Jean Marie was against me anyway.

THE DAY RNs were too serious for me, so, I tried to lighten up the atmosphere. When the nurse, Jean Nick, got pregnant, I put possible names on the board in the conference room. (Like Pick Nick, Saint Nick etc.) They were meant to be funny. Soon, I was using it to post many humorous lists like *To bee or not to bee* by Ruth Buzzy and Sting. It became a ritual. Someone would post a list daily.

Ann Marie Rowlette didn't like them at all. She erased the lists and sayings every day. It became a game. The nurses feared her and walked around like they were stepping on red-hot coals.

ONE MORNING, a frantic Jackie Sprawl greeted me at the door as I came in.

"Quick, Dr. Thek! Go to Trauma One! We have a nine-year-old boy who's barely breathing!"

That's strange! She's never lost her cool before.

I hurried to Trauma One Bay. There on the gurney was the nine-year-old boy just barely clinging to life. I looked at his pupils. They were blowing[2].

"Give me an ET tube[3]. We'll blow off some CO_2[4] and buy some time. In the meantime, get a CAT Scan."

I intubated him then hyperventilated him. The pupils returned to normal size.

"Any history?" I asked.

"Not much. His mother says he had a little headache last night. He went to bed early. This morning he was like this when she went in to get him ready for school."

After the boy had gone for the Scan, I asked, "Any family?"

Jackie said, "Just the mother."

"What's her name?"

"Ann Marie Rowlette."

"Come again. I thought you said Ann Marie Rowlette."

"I did."

Then I knew why Jackie was acting so strangely. Her boss had brought us her only son. But there was very little we could do.

This ain't gonna be easy.

She sat stoically in the grieving room expecting the worst. I'd been through this a hundred times before. It never got any easier. But now I knew the mother. I no longer saw her as my nemesis, the head of the nursing supervisors. She was now, Anne Marie Rowlette the vulnerable mother of a dying boy.

The boy survived for a few days. He had some kind of viral infection. Then he died. She, nor I, ever recovered. I never fought with her again. Without our knowing it, we each had become knitted together as family because we shared one another's grief.

40

EVENING SHIFT

E venings were very different from days. Some shifts were busy, and some were not. We hated hearing the sound of an approaching ambulance because of what it meant—more pain and work. Our fun counteracted the exposure to patients' complaints. It was like a shield and could deflect most drama.

Unlike the day shift, where you found married career nurses, many of the nurses on evenings were single and more carefree. You can choose to laugh or cry in the situations we witnessed. Some were hilarious, and some were tragic.

For instance, the evening the pretty brunette, Betty Anne Laguna, was at the front desk working triage. She hardly ever knew what was going on. Her mind was constantly distracted, in the stratosphere somewhere. But Betty Anne had a heart bigger than New York City.

The sliding glass door to the waiting room opened. A young man in his twenties entered, pointing a knife at the waiting patients. He says, "Stay where you are, or I'll stick you! Now gimme your money."

Most people would hide—not Betty Anne. She saw him threatening *her* patients. She came out from behind the counter to protect them. Positioning herself between them and the young man, Betty Anne held out her hand and authoritatively said, "Gimme that before you hurt someone. What would your mother say?"

The would-be assailant was so taken aback that he did hand her the knife! I wouldn't recommend that anyone do that, but it worked. Betty Anne defused the situation with her bold action.

She called the police. They arrived moments later and arrested the young man. Things returned to normal. The police were our friends and were always—and I mean always—there when we needed them.

THE BB GUN incident didn't fare as well.

The nurse, Melody Conley, frantically said, "Doctor Thek—hurry! We have a dead baby in Trauma One!"

She was always flying off the handle. I called her and her two nursing friends the Three Furies because they panicked at the slightest thing. That was not a good characteristic to have in the ER.

I dashed to Trauma Bay One and examined a baby boy, maybe three-months-old. Things were fast-paced. Perhaps it's better that way because we don't remember as much.

He was dead, having been shot with a BB gun. The entrance wound in the head was raised, meaning the firing was close.

"I swear the air rifle fell off the top shelf of the closet!" the mother insisted. "It was loaded and went off when it struck the floor. The BB hit my little boy."

"Where was the closet?"

"On the other side of the room."

She's lying. It couldn't have happened that way. Is the mother protecting someone, or did she do I herself?

I didn't see her again until we both went to the courthouse to plead his case. The witness before me was a so-called expert on air rifles.

"The rifle could keep its pressure for up to six months," he testified.

In other words, the shot could have happened the way the mother described. The court never called me, and she walked free.

I thought about that event a lot. Ultimately, we are not the Judge. Now I see that only GOD is, and HE will give everyone their due, either good or bad. We are commanded not to seek revenge in the Old Testament and the New[1]. Now, I must sometimes remember that there is no fooling HIM, no matter how many so-called "experts" are brought in. But then I thought she had gotten away with murder.

WE BECAME the dumping ground for everybody—the police, the doctors, the hospital. The ER was fully staffed and couldn't refuse anybody. When the hospital filled up (nearly every day), we held the overflow in the ER. RNs took orders from the doctors on the floors. They were not used to giving baths or medicines.

Dr. Rose was the director of the Family Practice Department. Technically, he was the medical head of the ER. Jackie and I met monthly with him, Sister, and other hospital bigwigs.. We never accomplished anything.

One early evening, a road crew was paving in a nearby town. A patient of Dr. Rose's lived on the street where they worked. A road-crew member wore the same shirt as he did. The patient left the house, but his wife stayed at home.

Hours went by. The crewman with the same shirt went into cardiac arrest. He fell into the tar and was unrecognizable. The wife thought it was her husband coming home. The paramedics began CPR, and the ambulance brought the man to our hospital.

Dr. Rose, one of the few GPs who ran a code, worked feverishly through the tar to resuscitate the man. "That's funny," he noted as he pumped on the patient's chest. "He's lost some weight."

Finally, the man was declared dead. Dr. Rose went to the wife in our grieving room.

"Come with me," he insisted.

What am I gonna do?

"C'mon. I wanna show you something," he said.

After going inside and shutting the door, Dr. Rose sat down next to her, taking her hand. I stood by the door. He began, "I'm sorry. We did everything we could, but your husband died."

"Oh, George," she wailed and started to cry, burying her head in

Dr. Rose's shoulder. She sobbed for fifteen minutes or so. Not just regular weeping; these were sobs, convulsing her whole body. Then, suddenly, it was over. She sat back and reached into her purse for a tissue. She dabbed her red eyes and blew her nose. Dr. Rose patted her on the back, and we left.

"They don't teach you how to comfort someone in medical school," he said as I went back to pick up a few waiting charts.

No, they don't. We should have a class. Comforting someone is one of the most important jobs we do.

After a while, she went home. Imagine her puzzlement when the woman saw someone waiting at the dining room table through the glass in the front door. He turned toward her as she opened the door. It was her husband! She fainted.

WE SAW all kinds of patients. Some with weird complaints for which I couldn't find a cause.

Once, a patient came in walking backward.

"Why are you walking that way?" I asked.

"If I knew, I wouldn't be here now, would I? I thought you could give me an answer." Insinuating that I was the crazy one.

"Who do you think I am, for goodness sake? I don't read a crystal ball! I have no idea why you walk backward!"

With that, he walked out of the room and ER backward. I guess he thought me stupid.

Another man brought in a brown paper bag. He removed a dead, white muskrat from it.

"What do you want me to do with it?" I asked.

"Does it have rabies?"

"Now, how do I know?"

"No need to get nasty."

The man turned and left, leaving me holding the bag in one hand and the dead muskrat in the other. All I could think of was *Muskrat Love* by Captain and Tennille[2].

THE MEDIA PEOPLE WERE A HOOT! They needed a filler story and wanted me to appear on television to tell asthmatics about the dangers of air conditioning. What dangers? If you know of any, please explain them to me.

Another time, TV wanted me to say a word about toothpick injuries. Someone had swallowed one and it perforated his bowel.

"Aren't seat belts a bigger issue?" I asked.

"No one will watch," the newsman replied.

"I'll be laughed out of Scranton if I talk about toothpicks!"

Ann Marie Rowlette had instructed me to be friendly with the media people, so it was necessary that I speak about toothpicks somehow.

"I'm sure there must be a story you can tell about toothpicks," the reporter said.

After a moment of silence, I thought, *That's what I'll say! The perfect story!*

I clapped my hands together. "I've got it!"

The newsman said, "Lights, camera, action."

A bit dramatic, don't you think?

"Now, look directly into the camera and speak."

Handing me a microphone, I began, "An auto driver was chewing on a toothpick. He didn't have his seat belt on. He hit another car and was flung up against the windshield. The driver swallowed the toothpick and busted his gut."

It never aired.

BETTY ANNE WAS a friend of Marilyn Carroll, another evening nurse. Marilyn was funny. She was always playing a practical joke on someone. One night, some of us decided to play one on her to even the score. Ben Bowden, a paramedic, became the ringleader.

"You know those popcorn pieces of Styrofoam that they pack things in?"

"Yeah," I answered, wondering where he was heading.

"Save 'em."

"Why?'

"Just do it."

Against my better judgment, I did. I saved them for a full six months. I had popcorn pieces in bags everywhere in my home.

"Get rid of them!" Edie yelled at me time and again.

Finally, Ben thought we had enough.

"Bring the bags in tonight."

"What are we gonna do?"

"Never you mind. Just meet me in the parking garage."

Why is he being so secretive? Guess he doesn't want us to know because we may not do it.

We met by Marilyn's car on the second story of the parking garage.

"Good. We have enough Styrofoam popcorn," Ben said, looking at all the bags.

"What are we gonna do with them?" I asked nervously.

"Fill up her car."

"What? How will we do that? How will we get inside? You're not gonna break in?"

"No, we do it with her keys."

"Now, how will you get her keys?"

Ben looked at his accomplice in crime, Steve Finn, another paramedic.

"We'll borrow them from her locker," Ben answered.

"'Borrow,' you mean 'steal,' don't you?"

"No, I mean 'borrow.' Steve will put them back before she ever knows they were missing."

"Me? Why me?" Steve asked. "I might get caught."

"It has to be you. You're the fastest one. Besides, her locker is small. You have small hands. They would fit."

There were all the bags of Styrofoam pieces. We had to act. Crossing over the street, we entered through the main doorway and viewed the nursing station of the ER while we stayed in the shadows —unseen.

Getting Marilyn's keys without her knowing it was virtually

impossible. She was in charge and viewed the locker room door from her post at the nurses' station. Every time Steve went to get the keys, he had to stop. Finally, she had to visit the jane.

Steve snuck into the locker room hurriedly. No one saw him lift the keys.

We took the keys across the street to the parking garage at the change of shift. We had to hurry while Marilyn and Betty Anne signed out. Marilyn had parked on the second floor of the parking lot, and her vehicle couldn't be seen from ground level. Steve approached the car and asked, "We can get in, but how do we get the Styrofoam inside?"

"Make a funnel out of cardboard. We'll pour it in through a crack in the back window," Ben answered.

That's what we did. A few cars passed us by, the drivers with looks of puzzlement on their faces. The Styrofoam pieces reached just above the dash.

"But she'll see it," I said.

"No, if we circle the car with industrial strength Saran Wrap first, she won't. Hurry, we only have a couple minutes to return the keys."

Steve left to replace the keys so Marilyn wouldn't suspect anything was amiss until she saw her car covered in Saran wrap. We hid behind other parked cars. When Marilyn entered the lot, she saw the Saran wrap around her vehicle and hastily removed it with the nurse's scissors Marilyn had. When she opened the front door, the popcorn pieces poured out.

We all had a good laugh at Marilyn's expense.

That should've been the end of it. But not with Marilyn and Betty Anne.

"I'll get those guys. Every time I turn on the heat, little pieces of Styrofoam fly out," she muttered repeatedly.

Months later, Marilyn did. Ben and Steve went to a conference in Allentown, about sixty miles away, and Ben told me about the adventure.

"Marilyn and Betty Anne followed us. I didn't see them. When we parked, they painted the car with watercolors. They were supposed to come out easily with a good car wash."

I almost heard Marilyn saying, "I'll get those guys."

"However, it wouldn't come out," he continued, "because I parked in the sun. The watercolors baked into the finish. When we returned, the car needed a new paint job."

That finished the practical jokes. They can be funny until someone loses an eye.

41

THE TRIP

Don Silvia was another nurse on evenings. He was about 5'9",
muscular, and had sparse hair. Don took great pride in being
part Portuguese. I had never met a Portuguese person
before, and we immediately became friends.

Don pulled me aside one night and said, "We need a fourth to go
on a golfing trip. Interested?"

There must be some golfing gene in doctors. Just mention a tee
time, and I'd be there.

"Count me in," I replied. "By the way, where is it?"

"Hilton Head."

"Excuse me, but isn't that in South Carolina?"

"Unless someone moved it."

Now how do I explain that to Edie? I know. I'll take her out to dinner!

We went to Cooper's Restaurant. It was a seafood place in Scranton
that she liked. Everything was going as planned until I mentioned
Hilton Head.

"Without me? How could you?"

She slammed her napkin on the table and went to the car, angrily
muttering as Edie left. You could have fried an egg on her head.

I followed a few minutes later, hoping that she would cool down. I might as well have chased the wind.

Opening the car door, she glared icily at me.

Uh-oh.

I got in behind the wheel of our tiny, blue Chevette and closed the door.

"I don't believe that you thought I could be bought with a lousy meal," she screamed as soon as the door was closed. "I should've known better."

"What's that supposed to mean!" I replied, getting angry myself.

"Oh …" she started to answer, then just looked out the window. I knew that further discussion was useless, so I silently drove home.

Well, that backfired. Maybe a lovely necklace.

The next day, I got up early and went to Deacon's, the jewelry shop. I bought it and went home. Leaving the necklace on our bed, I went two rooms over to my office. I heard the bedroom door slam. Edie emerged in a few moments.

She roared. "I'm not some whore that can be bought with some cheap jewelry!"

"Cheap? I spent a lot of money on that!" I said, my voice rising.

"Oh, I should … ."

"You should what?"

"Never mind."

We became silent as things settled down.

"That does it. I won't go," I said.

"No, no, no. I want you to go."

"You do? I thought you were against it."

"No, I think it's a good idea. I just don't like the way you asked me."

And she pecked me coquettishly on the lips. "Let's not fight about it anymore."

I embraced her and said, "I like this truce."

A few days later, as I prepared to get away, I noticed she had packed some of her things in a separate suitcase.

"Are you going somewhere?" I asked.

"To my parents' place to see them and my sister."

"Oh, now we see why you wanted to see me go."

"That's crazy. I just thought it would be a good time to go to Philly."

"Sure. Mighty coincidental."

"What did you expect me to do while you enjoy yourself?"

"What about the kids?"

"What about them? The boys can care for themselves for a few days, and Shannon can come with me."

I hated to admit it, but she was right. So, we each took our separate vacations. As I said, it was an omen.

In the morning, I carted my golf bag to the airport. Don Silvia was already there with the other two in our foursome, Jerry Donegal, the head of our excursion, and Scott Maris.

I shook hands with Jerry first. He was about 6'0" tall, the husband of one of the day nurses, and the owner of an ambulance. Scott was much shorter, maybe 5'6" with brown hair, and a brown mustache. He had on a big cowboy hat and boots. However, what stood out was his belt. It was a shiny leather with scales.

"What's that made of?" I said, pointing to his belt.

He smiled and said, "Snakeskin."

"Snakeskin? Why'd you get that?"

"If people can get alligator wallets, why not snakeskin belts?"

"Do you know from where on the alligator they get the skin to make the wallet?" Jerry asked.

Scott shook his head.

"The foreskin."

"The foreskin? Why do they do that?" Scott asked naively.

"So, if you rub it right, you turn a wallet into a suitcase."

With remarks like that, it's gonna be a long weekend.

We boarded the plane for Savannah. Don Silvia sat across the aisle while I sat beside Scott and Jerry. Don immediately fell asleep, something I should've done.

Once we were in the air, Jerry pointed to the belt. "If it rains, I wouldn't wear that if I were you."

"And why not?" Scott answered.

"Because water makes snakeskin shrink."

"Oh, come off it, it does not."

"Does, too. It's liable to choke you."

"Now, how's it gonna choke me? It's around my waist, not my neck."

"It could ride up."

"I'm glad I'm wearing boots. It's getting mighty deep in here."

"Are they snakeskin?"

"They are. Don't tell me they're gonna shrink, too.

"Yep. Won't be able to pull them off. They'll stick right to your skin."

"Oh, c'mon."

"Don't say I didn't warn you. Just ask other people who've worn snakeskin."

"You mean someone else wears snakeskin?" I blurted out before I censored my speech.

The other two looked at me as if I were crazy. Even the stunned Don Silvia lifted his head briefly before returning to la-la land. For the next two hours, we listened to stories from Jerry. I thought I had the gift of gab and could invent things anytime. I was nothing compared to Jerry. He never shut up—ever. And Jerry was the head of our adventure!

As we neared Savannah, he said, "Listen up, all of you. I had to tell a little white lie to play on the best courses. I expect all of you to back me up."

"What was it?" Scott asked.

"We're supposed to be four pros from Scranton."

"Golf pros?"

"Of course. That's what we're playing."

"Why, I just took it up a couple of weeks ago."

"Me too," Jerry admitted.

"They'll know we're not pros. All they have to do is take one look at us."

"What are they gonna do? Throw us out?"

"Maybe. I would. I didn't come all this way to be thrown off a golf course."

Jerry took his wallet out and placed it on the stand attached to the seat before him. "My money is as good as anybody's. If they want it, they'll let us play."

After we had landed at Savannah airport, we rented a car and drove to Hilton Head—less than an hour on back roads.

"Will you look at those trees?" Jerry asked as we drove along.

"What about them?' said Scott

"They're just loaded with Kudzu."

"Kudsoo? What's that?"

"It's a vine. It grows and grows and grows. It eventually strangles a tree."

We all looked closely, and indeed, some trees were already dying. *What Jerry said might be true.*

"Snakes like to live there," he continued.

"So?" Scott asked hesitantly.

"So, they smell snakeskin. They've been known to kill a man wearing it. Bite him right to death."

"Will you get off my belt?"

"Just saying."

"Well, keep it to yourself!"

"There are bees in there, too. They are attracted to snakeskin."

"Shut up already about the belt!"

There was quiet for a few seconds, then Jerry said, "Getting cloudy. Looks like rain."

"Look, will you stop if I wear a different belt?"

"What about the boots?"

"Don't have to worry about that. I wear golf shoes on the golf course."

"Golf shoes? What are they made of?"

"Leather."

Remembering a trip to the Adirondacks years before, I blurted out, "Leather! Can't wear that. Bears will smell it."

"Oh, that's just great! What then *can* I wear?"

"Sneakers," Jerry said.

"Sneakers!" Scott roared. "The starter will know I'm not a pro."

"Okay, okay. Wear your golf shoes, but stay away from the trees. That's where bears hang out."

We arrived at the condo shortly after that. It was a nice place. I shared a bedroom with Don Silvia. We unpacked hurriedly, and then we both went to bed. Traveling all day was tiring. We had to get rest for golf the next day.

Don fell asleep. I was glad he didn't snore.

Ah, peace and quiet.

In the morning, we ate some eggs and bacon we had gotten from a local convenience store. Then, we went to the golf course. Scott had dressed in a golfing outfit. He looked like Sammy Snead[1]. The starter took a second look at him but waved all of us onto the space between the first and tenth tees. The holes were "linked" together consecutively like a chain. Hence the term "Links." The fifth hole would turn us around. The ninth hole ended where the first began.

On the right side of this space were the first nine holes. On the left side were the next nine. When you were in the middle, no one could tell if you had played nine or eighteen.

Driving off the first tee, we hit one slice into the woods on the right and three hooks into the woods on the left. We were hackers. Scott had a seventy-two on the front nine.

"Not bad," I said loud enough for the starter to hear as we approached him, "Seventy-two." The starter looked at us askance. Then we proceeded on to the tenth hole.

Scott hit a ball into someone's basement. "What do I do now?"

"We're supposed to play it where it lies," Jerry answered.

"Even in someone's basement?"

"Especially there."

With that, Scott went into the basement. A few moments later, we saw a ball ricochet off the door and fall to the ground, bouncing out the open doorway. We heard Scott yell "Yes!" like Marv Alpert[2], oblivious that he was in someone's house. I guess a man's home is his castle until invaded by a golfer.

Scott emerged a few seconds later to hit the ball on its only flight on the right fairway.

"What did you do?" I asked after he rejoined us.

"The ball was in the middle of the room, so I whacked it. That was probably the best shot I had all day."

"Lucky the owner didn't shoot you," Don Silvia said.

"By the way, did you see my drive?" I asked.

"It went in the stream," Don answered.

"We should call your driver 'The Divining Rod' because you're always finding water," Jerry laughed.

At day's end, Scott had topped 140. None of us had even broken 100. But we had fun.

"That starter will never forget us," Don said.

Afterward, we went grocery shopping. Jerry took the wheel. Several young women in a red convertible pulled out from a side street and almost hit us, missing us by inches. The driver flipped *us* the bird. Jerry drove alongside the other car that was stopped at a red light. He rolled down the window.

"Is that the number of your legal parents?" Jerry asked.

The light turned green. The other vehicle peeled out while I looked for a place to hide.

We didn't play any better on the other courses the next two days. One was by the ocean. On the third hole was a giant sand trap off the tee to the right. It had a spiked wall with cattails at the other end that you had to clear. The trap was nearly 200 yards long. I took one long look at the trap.

It's much shorter to go over it but safer to the left. That's something you play away from.

I hit my tee shot to the left and away from the trap.

"Bruck-bruck-bruck," Scott clucked. He teed up his ball second and aimed right over the trap. "Let me show you how it's done."

Naturally, like iron being attracted to a magnet, he went right into the sand.

"Is that how it's done?" Jerry asked, teeing up his ball and hitting it left.

Scott grew red-faced.

He tried to hit over the spikes wall, but the ball would invariably hit them and bounce back into the sand. Cursing must've been invented on a golf course. Every time the ball would returned to him, Scott would curse again. After five failed attempts, he hit the ball the other way, back towards the tee.

"The green's the other way," Jerry laughed.

"Oh, shut up!" an angry Scott retorted.

THEN IT WAS BACK to Scranton and reality. On the fight back, I didn't sit near them. As a result, it was quiet, and I slept.

42

NIGHT SHIFT

T hen there was the night shift. Both the patients and the staff were unique. We had our regulars; the nurses would swear they all came when the moon was full.

"Where's your evidence?" the skeptic in me would ask.

"Everybody knows that," Jean Marie Ziforski, one of our nurses, would say.

"I'm not 'everybody.'"

She'd throw up her hands and walk away.

I remember some patients. There was Ralph and his significant other, Judy. They'd come in around three a.m. I suspect because they couldn't sleep. On schedule one night, Ralph and Judy strolled into an empty ER.

Jean Marie escorted them into an examining room.

"Why are you here?" I asked while closing the door.

"The FCC is after me," Ralph replies.

"The Federal Communications Commission?"

"No, the Federal Cheese Commission."

"What makes you think that?"

"Every time I try to go to sleep, I smell cheese. It's driving me crazy."

Judy spoke up, "You're already crazy."

"Like you!" he roared.

"At least I can prove it. I have the papers right here!"

With that, she reached into her purse and withdrew some signed papers. "Now, whose signature is that?" Judy asked, pointing to the bottom of the page.

"Whoa!" I shouted, getting between them, "Take your argument outside. You want to know where the cheese smell comes from, right?"

"Right."

"Where do you put your sneakers at night?"

"Under the bed."

"Put them in the closet."

Judy started to laugh.

"What's so funny?" Ralph asksed her.

"That's just what I said."

That continued their argument. After they left, I went to the waiting room and got a few chairs.

"Where are you going with those?" Jean Marie asked.

"Entertainment," I answered, opening the electric door and going outside.

We sat on the chairs under the ambulance overhang and watched Ralph on one corner yell at Judy, who was catty-corner to him. She yelled back. They were both oblivious to the time of day, and someone turned on the lights behind them. They continued for fifteen minutes

"I've got proof you're crazy right here!" Again, she'd go to her purse and remove the papers.

Finally, he said, "I just love you when you're mad."

She stopped yelling abruptly. They each went to the corner between them and embraced.

I picked up my chair. Jean Marie said, "You're missing the good part."

"Show's over for tonight. Tomorrow's another day."

Another night, there was a patient in Room 7, our ENT[1] room. As I walked back, I looked at the chart. Her chief complaint was she had an ant stuck on her uvula.

Now, how did it get there?

"I was drinking some soda, you know," the teenage girl sitting in the examining chair said nonchalantly. She wore pierced earrings everywhere: her nose, lips, eyelids, and tongue. Getting them must have hurt.

"I took a big gulp. As I did, I saw this big old ant on top of the soda, swimming fast, you know, fighting to stay alive. It was too late to stop swallowing. So, I swallowed, you know. When I did, he hung on to this thing in my throat that hangs down, you know." And with that, she opened her mouth and pointed to her uvula. I looked inside, and there, stuck to her uvula, was the dead ant. I thhought of *The Pink Panther* theme, "Dead ant. Dead ant. Dead ant, dead ant, dead ant ... " I removed it.

As I did so, I thought of the ant. He or she must have seen the soda gush down the esophagus toward the stomach and clutched the uvula for dear life.

What a way to die!

The next patient was a teenager with an orange rash on her face.

"I swear, it's real!" the mother exclaimed as I entered the room.

Hmm, never saw an orange rash before.

I took an alcohol wipe and rubbed on it. The rash disappeared.

A flabbergasted mother shouted at the daughter, "But you said you didn't use the markers!"

I never uttered a word and left.

IT WAS fun to work nights with the nurse Jean Marie. I never knew what to expect. One night, I was sitting at the table in our windowed conference room across a hallway from the nurses' station when she came in and plopped in a chair across from me. "I'm so tired. It reminds me of when I was eight months pregnant and ate a whole watermelon."

I looked up. To understand what I told her, you must know about Pitocin. It's a medicine called "Pit" given by IV to induce labor. Also, everybody knows watermelons have little bugger pits waiting for a good chomp to ruin teeth. So, I began, "Didn't your doctor tell you not to eat watermelons?"

"No. Why?"

"Because that's where 'Pit' comes from."

She was gullible and believed me. However, that night Jean Marie looked up Pitocin. It isn't extracted from watermelons. We had a good laugh and thought the matter was closed.

A year and a half went by. At four a.m., I sat across from Jean Marie in the conference room. Judy Penny, another R.N., seven and a half months pregnant, came in and sat next to her. "I'm so tired, I could eat a whole watermelon," Judy commented.

That caught my attention and I looked up. Jean Marie said, "I swear, I never told anyone about our conversation about 'Pit.'"

Another year and a half went by. Dr. Sleck, from Ob-Gyn, came to the ER one night on his way home after repairing an episiotomy I'd made. He claimed angrily, "All the nurses on the floor are telling the patients to eat watermelons. If I ever catch the person who started that rumor, I'll – I'll kill him."

I didn't say a word.

Another year and a half passed. As was often the case, I had to deliver a baby. I didn't recognize the mother. After the birth, Jean Marie informed me she was a nurse on the O.B. floor.

"I ate a whole watermelon last night," she told me. "I know it caused my labor."

I couldn't argue with a new mother, so I threw up my hands and left the room. I gave up. Pitocin does come from watermelon pits.

As an addendum, years later, Danielle (more on her later) was having her first baby. Because the father was MIA[2], I went to Nesbitt Hospital to help. It was about twenty miles from Mercy. On the wall of Labor and Delivery was a picture of watermelons. That's how "wives'" tales begin.

∽

ANOTHER NIGHT, I was behind a patient asking him to take a deep breath. Jean Marie was stationed at his front. He didn't inhale. I had the stethoscope on the back of his chest, listening.

"Breathe in and out," I ordered.

Still no sound. Jean Marie laughed.

"Breathe in and out!"

She became hysterical. I had to see what was so funny, so I went in front of the patient. He was taking his *teeth* in and out! The expression on the patient's face showed that he thought I was crazy while she continued laughing.

WE PUT urine samples in little, clear plastic cups. One night, Jean Marie was busy in another room. I ushered a groaning man into a room. The patient appeared to have a kidney stone by the tint of his urine. He continued to moan.

Iced tea looks like bloody urine, so I put some in a container. Finally, Jean Marie came out to where I had the filled cup. The man moaned on cue.

"What's his problem?" she asked.

"I think he has a kidney stone."

I took his urine sample container, removed the lid, and sniffed.

"I don't think he's diabetic."

Then, I drank it.

Her color was as white or whiter than the sheet on the gurney. Jean Marie passed out, hitting the floor. She wasn't hurt, or I'd be in deep "doo-doo." She was gullible.

SOMEBODY ON NIGHTS was stealing our food. You can take other things, but don't mess with our lunches. We were upset about it, but we couldn't figure out who would do such a thing. The perp always stayed one step ahead of us—avoiding all our baited traps. That's when GOD entered and helped us find the culprit.

One night, a patient brought in a dead snake.

"Why did you bring that here?"

"To see if it's poisonous,"

"It doesn't have pits, so it's not poisonous."

We finished eating a pizza, put the dead snake in the box, and promptly forgot about it.

A couple of hours later, I called in the cardiologist. I was busy suturing when I heard him scream. Nobody touched our food again.

KAREN LOFTON, another night nurse, made me laugh.

"It never rains at night," she stated.

"What!" I exclaimed.

"No, clouds only come out during the day."

Another night, Karen asked, "Why do we rotate tires? Don't they rotate themselves?"

And she was a nurse!

I LIKED WORKING nights at Mercy. Fewer bosses around, there was less patient load, and I did what I wanted. That's also the time when the crazies come in. People like me.

We saw many social problems. Once a lady was found sitting on a park bench at eleven-thirty p.m. She had disembarked from a Wilkes-Barre bus. I don't know how the woman boarded because she couldn't talk. The police brought her to (Where else?) the ER.

The woman communicated by pointing to different letters of the alphabet on a card she carried with her. I didn't have time to put the letters together, so I rifled through her handbag to get information. I found her daughter's phone number inside and called it.

"Who is this?" a woman answered gruffly.

"It's Dr. Thek from Mercy, Scranton, and your mother—"

"How did you get my number?"

"Well, from—"

Slam went the receiver! For a moment, I was as speechless as the mother.

This must be very odd for her. First, she's in a strange city at night, and then the daughter hangs up. Very peculiar!

About a half-hour went by. A policeman, called Officer Radly, phoned and asked, "How did you get that number?"

What is it about this number?

"It was easy. I just went through the mother's pocketbook."

Silence. Finally, Officer Radly admitted, "We've been after the daughter for seven years. When your nurse called us a few minutes ago, our detectives put two and two together. We need that number."

"I'll give it to you, but I doubt she'll answer. Been scared off."

"We'll try anyway."

I was amazed. I was with the mother for a couple of minutes, and I spoke with her daughter, who was wanted for a crime. The police had come up empty after seven years. I was part detective, too!

Should receive a salary from the police.

We sent the lady to stay at her sister's. And that ended our involvement.

I often felt sorry for patients. One night, a redheaded drunk came in. I discovered he was a veteran, so I let him sleep on the gurney, and we ordered a taxi to take him home through our Social Services in the morning. The drunk promptly took it and robbed a bank. What a plan! It was so unusual that initially, he got away with it. However, later that day he was arrested.

Will I get to join him in jail? It will come out that I gave him the ride. Am I an accomplice?

All the next day I expected the telephone to ring from the police. I was relieved when they never called.

43

SUSIE

We had many volunteers in the ER. We called them "candy stripers." As I recall, they were usually young women on their way to being nurses. Occasionally, we had a male, but for the most part, they were high school girls. They dressed in pink candy cane outfits and did odd jobs like delivering mail. They were trying to pad their résumés. I knew the drill well.

One stood out among the rest. Susie was her name. She was a simple young woman who always smiled. Susie was not interested in a career as a nurse.

That's good because she don't have the smarts for the job anyway.

Susie was short, maybe five feet tall. But, like my mother, she was not so little that her feet didn't touch the floor, at least when they walked. Susie was plain-looking, not at all beautiful like some of the other volunteers. But there was something about her. She had a genuine smile that, as Tolstoy observed, made any face beautiful. With Susie around, you didn't need lights. She lit up any room she was in with her bright smile.

We always had various excreta in the department. The smell was outrageous—especially GI bleeds and vomit. I remember once when a patient couldn't make it to the bathroom. She urinated right in the hallway.

Her nurse, Betty Anne, asked, "Urine?"

The woman replied, "Of course it's mi—une!"

I almost lost it. I had to take a time-out and go to the conference room. Marilyn Carroll was there along with Susie, who was busily mopping the floor.

"Looks like someone peed in the hallway," I said upon entering.

"At least it's not *#*#," Marilyn said as Susie continued to mop the linoleum in the conference room.

"Someone has to clean it up."

"Well, don't look at me. It's not my turn."

With that, Susie asked energetically, "Can I do it?"

I looked at Marilyn, who said to her, "Why not? You *do* realize that it stinks."

Susie was beside herself with joy. She put on plastic gloves, took her bucket, left the conference room, and mopped the hallway.

I looked quizzically at Marilyn. She shrugged her shoulders and said, "To each their own."

From then on, whenever there was something to be cleaned up that the nurses didn't want to do, Susie would do it—especially the toilets. The odor in the ER vanished. For a change, it smelled good and clean.

It was "beneath" doctors to clean up a mess. The old saw claims that *#*# flows downhill, so it became the nurses' responsibility. They, in turn, passed it on to Susie. She was ecstatic to oblige. Soon the nurses were leaving things for her to clean up.

When a code was over, there was usually excreta everywhere. Nobody wanted to tidy the mess—except for Susie[1]. She would beam a smile whenever we called her name to help. There was no job beneath her.

Then one night, just before 11:00, when we'd be off duty, the radio blared. "We have a multiple-car MVA[2]," the excited paramedic said, "One death, seven injured— over."

It was against protocol for a paramedic to pronounce someone dead. So, I asked, "What makes you think they're dead? Over."

"If your head wasn't attached to your body, wouldn't you be?

Over."

I thought about the situation quickly, then said, "Okay. Take two to CMC, two to Moses Taylor. The other three here—over."

"Oh, *#*#," one of the Furies yelled when I was off the radio. "We don't have room!"

"Make room!" I replied.

"Looks like a long night tonight!" another Fury said.

"Somebody, call my wife!" I shouted amid the chaos. At least, that's the way it looked to the untrained eye. But it wasn't chaos at all. We knew exactly what was going on.

One of the nurses handed me a phone. It was ringing on the other end.

"Hello?" Edie answered. "This can't be good at this time of night."

"It's not. I'll be very late tonight."

"What else is new?"

"New York, New Jersey, New—"

"Oh, shut up, wise guy. This is getting very old."

"Look, it's not my fault that there was an accident. Someone has to pick up the pieces," I said with my voice rising.

"But that someone doesn't have to be you."

"I don't have time for this!"

"You're running out of time!"

I slammed down the receiver.

"Trouble in paradise?" nurse Marilyn Carroll asked.

Before I could answer, the paramedics arrived with the three patients.

We got involved with replacing or starting IVs. I was busy with procedures. Dom Rufalo was there now for the night shift and he pitched in. Nobody thought of overtime. We just did what had to be done.

There were tubes everywhere. Chest tubes, ET[3] tubes, NG[4] tubes, urinary catheters—you name it. We used them.

We made many phone-calls home to waiting spouses or significant others that night.

Anyway, the evening shift stayed until things settled down. Dominic followed me, and we worked well together in clearing the department. It took almost two hours, but gradually the excitement subsided, and the ER became nearly quiet. All I could think of was going home.

As usual, Susie was busy with her bucket. We had almost finished at about 1:00 when she tugged on my white coat.

"Yes, Susie, what is it?"

"I missed my bus. Can you take me home?"

"Be happy to. Give me a couple minutes to sign out to Dr. Rufalo."

After signing out, she followed me to the street beside the hospital. I parked there because the lot was often full when I came on duty in the afternoon. We each got into my Chevette. I put the key in and turned the ignition—nothing. I turned it again—still nothing.

Susie started praying out loud. "Dear LORD, please make it work."

Just then, two seedy-looking characters—one with black hair, one with blond— approached the car.

Oh great! What are they gonna do to us? Maybe a stick-up.

Then I looked at Susie.

No matter what, I have to defend her.

The black-haired man tapped on my window. Against my better judgment, I rolled it down.

"We hope you don't mind," he began, "But you left your lights on this afternoon when you parked. We had to take your battery out of the car to turn them off. We've been waitin' on the front porch for you to come out."

"All this time?"

He nodded.

"That must've been over ten hours!"

"Had nothin' to do anyway."

Had them pegged all wrong. Have to be more careful with the lights.

I exited the car and popped the hood. They hooked up the battery like pros. I slid in behind the wheel again and turned the key. The engine purred.

"Want to give you something for your time," I said, still amazed that they had waited all evening.

"Nah."

"But I wanna do something."

He thought for a moment and then remarked, "Okay, the next time we're sick, treat us for nothin'."

"Deal," and we shook on it.

After driving about a mile, Susie said, "GOD answered my prayer."

"How?"

"Those two guys and the battery."

"You heard them. They waited for me all evening. It has nothing to do with God."

"It didn't?"

We became silent as we left Scranton and headed north toward Clarks Summit. Susie lived in an apartment complex near my house—maybe a mile away.

Halfway there, Susie looked out the window. Trees along the road swayed in the night breeze. Susie was looking toward them when she started to cry.

"Why are you doing that?" I asked.

Susie reached in her pocketbook for a tissue. As she turned away from the window, I could see her moistened face in the glow of the street lamps. She blew her nose, then said while sniffling, "Grew up—here. It's gonna be hard—to leave."

"Leave?"

"That's what a girl does—when she gets married."

"Married?"

"Thought you knew that. Guess not."

"Married?"

"Yep, marriage. Do you know when a man and a woman love each other and live together? Don't they teach that in your highfalutin schools?"

"Just never thought *you'd* get married," I blurted out before I could censor my remark.

"Why not? Because I'm slow? I I know how to please a man," she said matter-of-factly. Some women would be angry—not Susie.

I must've blushed.

"Why are you turnin' red?" she asked as we passed under a street lamp by the big bridge for the Turnpike and started up the hill toward Clarks Summit.

"I didn't mean it like that," I said defensively, but that *was* what I meant. Wanting to change the subject, I asked, "What makes you think God was involved back there?"

"All I know was that I prayed one minute, and these two men showed up the next."

"Coincidence," I replied, trying to show her how smart and sophisticated my thinking was.

Why am I trying to impress her?

She looked at me as if to say, "Are you kiddin'?"

I pulled into the parking lot of Susie's apartment complex.

"When's the big day?" I asked.

"Next month, June 6th."

She got out of my Chevette. I waited until I knew she was inside—an old habit.

Most of my thoughts were about the ER on the way to my house.

I wondered, *What will it be like without Susie? We'll miss her, but we'll return to our old ways.*

But as I pulled into our driveway, my last thought was, *It was a coincidence, wasn't it?*

The truth was I envied her simple faith. I had yet to realize it was available to everyone.

As usual, I had already blotted out the night's event concerning the car accident. But I couldn't help but think about Susie.

I entered the dark house and trudged upstairs to the bedroom—physically exhausted. Edie was fast asleep.

I looked down at her and wondered *Susie, do you know what you're getting into?*

Getting undressed, I rolled back the cover on my side and got into bed.

I didn't realize it yet, but this stiff-necked, stubborn heart of mine was changing. Like parched soil receiving the rain, it was being softened, so it could receive the WORD. I couldn't be convinced that JESUS is the Messiah by arguments. I couldn't be convinced by fear. GOD knew that, so HE sent Susie to show me what it really means to be a Christian.

44

THE AHA

I met the orderly on the night shift at work, Bob Eckert. He was strong, about 5'9", with reddish brown hair. He and I hit it off immediately.

"If I could only lose five pounds," he continually said whenever we slowed down enough to sit at the conference room table to chat.

"But you're not fat," I'd note.

"Now. Don't want to end up like my father."

"What happened to him?"

"He had a heart attack while in the saddle and died."

"That's the way to go," I said. "Quick. At least he was happy." That was how I thought then— wine, women, and song.

Nancy, a diminutive, no-nonsense night nurse, was carrying his child.

"I just hate practical jokes," she often said.

Of course, I had to pull some on her. We put cellophane under the toilet seat and KY jelly on the mouthpiece for the phone. I dialed the hospital number. She answered, and the KY smeared all over her face.

She saw red. "Why I'll ... "

She went to the bathroom to clean up. In a few minutes, her scream echoed down the hallways. Nancy emerged with her pants wet.

"Don't eat the yellow snow," I snickered.

"Oh … " she wanted to swear, thought better of it, and stomped away.

Bob and I drove to climb Mt. Marcy in New York in October 1984. My car was small, a Chevette with a stick shift.

When I caught a glimpse of the mountain from the Northway, I asked, "Is that snow at the top?"

"Sure is."

"I don't have snowshoes."

"We'll make it, somehow."

After the drive, we hiked in. Bob and I set up camp by the river where the student had thrown in his wallet years before. I knew the spot. We pitched our two-person pup tent.

Out of nowhere, a ranger appeared. "Do you have a permit?" he asked.

"I've been camping out here for years and never needed a permit!"

"No permit, then you'll have to go tomorrow. It's too late to leave tonight. I'll let you stay the night," and he turned to leave.

"Thanks," I replied sarcastically.

He stopped and turned back toward me. He pointed his finger and said, "A wise guy, I see."

Better keep my big mouth shut before he throws us out of here.

Bob intervened, "We're deeply appreciative," he said calmly, his words oozing submission.

"That's better," the ranger said and went his way.

After he had gone, Bob turned to me and said, "What *are* you doing?"

"He's a jerk!"

"I don't care if he is! He has the power to make us leave. We don't want to get him mad."

"But—"

Bob held up his hand. "No 'But's. All I want is a good night's sleep. If I have to lick his boots a little, I will."

I realized he was right.

Climbing Mt. Marcy.

The world is changing, and not always for the better.

We retired early and tried to sleep. I accidentally kicked down the pole. The tent collapsed. I couldn't get up, so Bob turned on the lantern to see.

"What happened?" he asked.

"My leg went into spasm. I guess it was the long ride."

He erected the pole again and yelled, "It's like an ice cube out here!"

Bob left the lantern burning for its heat.

"That lantern will use up all the oxygen in the tent, and we'll suffocate," I insisted. "Or it could start a fire."

"You worry too much. Would you rather freeze?" he asked as he left the lantern on.

As soon as Bob dozed off, I extinguished it. Then, I followed him into sleep.

Light awakened me.

"What *are* you doing?" I asked.

"I'm relighting the lantern. Somehow it went out."

As soon as he dozed off again, I put the lantern out and tried to sleep myself. When I dozed off, Bob would light the lantern. Neither of us slept at all.

In the morning, Bob and I discovered that it snowed sixteen inches on the top of Mt. Marcy. We started the hike anyway. We hadn't come from Scranton to be foiled by a "little" snow!

On the trail, we ran into a French woman from Montreal. She looked at my sneakers and said, "You vill nev-er make it in those," she said in a thick French accent while pointing at my feet.

She was correct; we should've turned back. But I perceived it as a challenge. Now come what may, I was going to make it, regardless of my footwear.

Who is she to tell me that I won't make it?

On the trail, Bob and I were huffing and puffing. Two men passed us. They spoke the whole time like this was a walk in the park or something.

It's bad enough they can talk, but they're speaking French! This is America!

Then, I realized that Canada is America too. The Adirondacks are closer to Montreal than New York City, even though Mt. Marcy is the highest mountain in New York State. Anger doesn't know reason, remaining foreign to it.

We hiked and hiked—trying to avoid the snow was impossible. Finally, we reached the top. The snow was easily over the sides of my sneakers. I took them off to rest.

I should've worn boots.

We traversed a small wooden bridge over a running stream on the descent. Bob, in his boots, had no problem. He crossed, but I, now back in my sneakers, slipped on the bridge and fell into the stream!

I jumped out and ran down the trail, where an astonished Bob caught me.

"Why are you running and wet?" he asked.

"I f-fell c-crossing the s-stream," I shivered.

"I didn't see. I was looking ahead. C'mon, and you'll dry off as we walk."

I checked, and there were no breaks. Only my pants were wet, as the creek wasn't too deep. Bob was right, and they soon dried while we hiked.

"We should break camp," I said upon our return. "Don't want that ranger to pay us another visit. Besides, it's cold."

"But it's three miles down, and I'm tired."

"Just put one foot in front of the other and go."

"Let's go to a motel," he suggested warming to the idea. "We could each take a hot bath."

"Sounds good."

We trudged the three miles out. Up and down, up and down we went.

"One more hill," I'd say. But at the top of the hill was always another valley. We'd continue to be disappointed it wasn't the end of what we considered an ordeal. The backpacks chafed us. Our muscles didn't want to obey our brains. Then, another hill appeared.

"This time, I mean it. One more hill," I said.

"Oh, shut up! If I hear that one more time, I'll kill you!"

We finally reached the bottom as the sun set. Nothing was sweeter than that! I was too tired to say anything, which, for me, was saying something.

Driving to a motel, we each took baths. Bob went first. They had a TV, and I watched as the San Diego Padres lost the World Series to the Detroit Tigers. Then, I took my bath. The water soothed my aching bones. By the time I finished, I heard him snoring.

THE FOLLOWING FALL, Bob and I went with Tom Major, two security guards, and three paramedics to climb Mt. Washington in New Hampshire. It was my third time there, so I became the expert.

"We should go up Tuckerman's Ravine on the south side, away from the wind."

It was a good plan. But we neglected the time difference up North. The sun sets earlier than it had in Scranton.

We stayed at a lodge, and in the morning, we left early. Upon reaching the top, Tom stated, "I want to see the lake down here." He pointed it out to me on the map

"I don't think it's a good idea," I replied. "You don't know this mountain. I do. It's very fickle at this time of year, and it's getting late. We should go back."

"I tell you what. Let's put it to a vote."

Against my better judgment, we did. Five wanted to see the lake, while two others and I thought it a good idea to return.

"Why don't we compromise?" Tom asked. "You go down this trail, and we'll see the lake over here," he pointed at the map. "You wait for us where the paths intersect."

"Okay," I agreed.

Two paramedics and I started down the mountain. The other five took off for the lake. Upon reaching the point where the paths crossed, we stopped and waited. Then, the clouds came, rolling over rocks like waves. It became windy and cold.

"I think we should go, or else we'll get caught in a fog bank," one of the paramedics said.

"That's not a good idea." I countered. "The others will wait and get caught in the dark."

"So what? They wanted to see that stupid lake."

"But someone could get injured. We would never know it, and he would die. I don't think we should split up."

"We already have."

I had conveniently forgotten leaving my cousin, Tommy, on the trail while Johnny and I went ahead in the snowstorm on my first expedition there.

"We gave our word to wait, and that's what I'll do," I stated firmly.

"Even if it means dying."

"Yes," I answered firmly but was torn apart inside.

"For another five minutes, I'll wait, then I'm outta here," the paramedic said.

I settled for that. GOD had the five arrive in less than five minutes. I don't know what I would have done if it had been longer.

"How was the lake?" I asked as we started the descent.

"You mean the puddle," Tom tried to laugh.

GOD must look down on us and shake HIS head. We go off on tangents when we should not. If we stick to the path HE has laid out, everything will be fine. If we stray, anything could happen. We are in a lot of trouble if we depend on our wits. At that time, I didn't know GOD. Therefore, we got into trouble. Thankfully, HE's merciful and intervened.

It grew dark while we went down the mountain.

"Where are we?" I asked.

"Lost," replied one of the paramedics.

"We are not," a security guard insisted. "I know perfectly well where I am."

"And where is that?" the paramedic asked.

"Right here."

"Very funny. But how are we gonna get out of these woods?

"Beats me."

Just then, we saw a flashlight of some other late hikers bobbing along the path.

"C'mon," I said. "Let's follow it."

We kept the light ahead of us, tripped, and fell a few times but got out eventually. GOD taught me that I should always follow that inner voice even if it is whispered or other people disagree. It can be viewed as stubbornness. I prefer to think of it as tenacity. There are times to compromise and other times to hold your ground. I was learning.

That trip became important because that's when I invented the AHA (Alphabet Hikers of America). We climbed yearly high peaks that were above the timberline. The mountains had to begin with different letters of the alphabet.

"Does 'Half Dome' count as an 'H' or 'D?'" I asked Bob.

"Oh, I don't know! You started the stupid club. You can make its rules."

"Then I'll make it an 'H' and a 'D' because I've climbed it twice."

"Oh, brother!"

Bob was right. Because I created the club, I could make any rules I pleased. GOD has the same right as the Creator. That's what 'sovereign' means[1].

We often overlook that. We want things *our* way and use Him like a puppet to get what *we* want. But it doesn't work that way. GOD will bless America if HE wants to, not because we want HIM to. When does HE do it? Simple, when we obey HIM.

"We have to make some allowance for mountains that begin with the same letter, like Mt. Marcy and Mt. Mitchell," I said.

"Shut up already about the AHA!" Bob replied.

"Maybe we can substitute one letter for another if we've climbed two beginning with the same letter."

Bob stuffed cotton in his ears.

45

EDUARDO

E duardo Ciani, an orderly from work who took Bob Eckert's old job, was trying to get into medical school.

He never got in but had to settle for Physician Assistant's school.

Unfortunately, Eduardo had some trouble with his wife, Sheryl. He moved in for a couple of weeks, taking Kathryn's old room. How was I to know Eduardo would return? Or that the second time he would stay for six months?

~

EDUARDO LOVED BASEBALL. At games, he was a heckler.

"Hey, ump! Your momma wears combat boots!"

I tried not to pay attention.

"Hey, ump! Your sister does tricks in New York!"

The umpire turned around and stared at me. I avoided eye contact with the ump all the time, thinking *Would rather sit on hot coals than go to another ballgame with Eduardo.*

But he insisted on going often. One time, he won something there and was put on the field. Eduardo had to run to first base and beat a throw.

"You're out!" the umpire yelled.

"I was safe!"

"No, you were out!"

Eduardo poked the ump in his chest protector, and they escorted Eduardo off the field. He returned to his seat.

"That stupid ump! I was safe." It wasn't even a real game!

Eduardo yelled, "Your wife goes out with your best buddy while you ump the game!"

It was a long night.

I took him golfing many times. Through him, I became addicted to naming the Top Ten of everything.

"Name the ten greatest bands," he said while we played.

"The Beatles, the Stones ... " I said as I swung the driver on the tee. When I finished on the third hole, he said, "Now, name the ten greatest solo artists."

"Male or female?"

"Both."

"Elton John, Billy Joe, Neil Diamond ... Barbra Streisand, Bette Midler, Janis Joplin ... "

"Now, the ten greatest baseball players," he said.

"Babe Ruth, Ty Cobb, Joe DiMaggio, Ted Williams ... "

"How about the ten greatest basketball players?"

"Bill Russell, Bob Cousy, Larry Bird, Ron Kornegay—"

"Whoa! Stop right there. Ron, who?"

"Kornegay. He was only 5'6" tall—"

"Hold it! Five six? And he played basketball?"

"Not only played but was great at it! He could dribble, shoot, and pass better than anybody. He went to Southside High School in Newark. When he was there, they would turn off the gym lights and shine a spotlight on the doorway. He would come in dribbling. It was something to see. A real work of art. He went on to score over 2500 points in college."

"Where did he go?"

"Monmouth."

Eduardo snorted. "Monmouth! Where's that? It's not exactly UCLA."

"Still, 2500 points is a ton of points wherever you play."

He thought for a moment, then said, "What do you consider 'great?' I noticed you left off Dr. J and Wilt Chamberlin from your list. Is it a black thing?"

I laughed. "Bill Russell was black. So was Ron Kornegay."

"Then what do you consider 'great?'"

I hit the ball off the sixteenth tee. After a brief pause, I said, "It's one thing to be great yourself. It's quite another to make others around you great."

"Like Bill Russell!"

"Exactly."

After a few moments, Eduardo asked, "How did Ron Kornegay make others great?"

"By passing them the ball when he couldn't score, and they could."

I swung the club again, and the ball jumped off the last tee.

ON OTHER OCCASIONS, Eduardo and I discussed marriage and family often.

"Parents should stick together for the sake of the children," he'd say.

"What if they fight? Should the children be subjected to that?"

At the time, I thought divorce was an option. The truth is GOD hates divorce.[1]

We thought at the time that love was an emotion. It's not. Love is a virtue, and we can work on it as such. It took years, and my brain bleeds to realize that, but I changed.

EDUARDO TAUGHT me how to make authentic enchiladas and tacos. They are still a part of my diet. His mother is from Mexico, and he's from Albuquerque. Homemade tamales came in the mail.

Eduardo eventually returned to his wife. I think it was because of their daughter, Kendall. They went on to have a son.

We are supposed to work things out.

46

THE OFFICE

We had six ER-trained docs and one internist, probably the only hospital in the country with that many. The administration didn't know how good they had it. Each of us was excellent, but all good things must end.

First, Dom and Phil opened up a successful practice. They shared one full-time position between them. That corroborated what Sister thought of the ER being a stepping stone. Then, we lost two more docs. The edifice we built was crumbling. I wanted to evacuate before becoming part of the rubble.

"Why don't you come in with Phil and me?" Dom asked. "We could use you."

"Like the idea of having a practice that no one can mess with."

"Then it's settled."

"Whoa! I didn't say that. You've established your practice. I haven't. In effect, I'd be working for you. Although your offer is generous, I have to decline. I'm not ready."

A couple of months went by. Another doctor left. I was ready now. Then Doctor Major made an appointment to come over to my house.

Wonder what this is about?

We exchanged pleasantries and then retired to the patio.

After we had sat, Tom looked at me pensively and asked, "Want to go in practice with me? I need a partner."

So, that's what he wants.

Then I realized *we are equals. I have to get out of the ER. I can't think of a person I'd rather be partners with.*

My answer was almost immediate. "Deal." And, we shook on it.

I stopped being the director of the ER but still worked there.

We established our office three towns over in Olyphant. Tom and I rented the office from the Russian church through one of the security guards. We painted it and hired an interior decorator for the curtains and furniture, spending many afternoons together preparing to open our own office.

We bought a computer for billing and record keeping. Everything was changing, and computers were becoming necessary tools to conduct business. Something is lost in the transition from the hands-on approach, but I was oblivious to that. All I wanted to do was care for people. There's more to it than that, but having a shingle outside with your name on it makes it all worthwhile—almost. Pride had reared its ugly head. I puffed out my chest.

Mom and Dad would be proud of me.

We hired a secretary named Margaret O'Malley. Her name was an instant hit with me. Her looks didn't hurt either. She was tall with brown hair. She presented well. We should've checked her references, but we were so busy painting that we didn't.

Finally, the big day arrived. I was alone as Tom was working in the ER. When I was done, I would go to the ER in the evenings, and Tom would take over the office. They were sixteen-hour days, but we were young.

Everything was new, right down to the linoleum. I was excited, and now I was an entrepreneur.

My first patient was a little old lady there to have her blood pressure checked.

I took her to a room and put the cuff around her arm

Hmm. 150/86. Not bad for her age.

"You don't need medication. Your blood pressure will be great if you lose a few pounds." I said honestly.

"Are you callin' me fat?"

I blushed. One thing I learned was *never* to call a woman fat.

"No, no, no," I apologized profusely. "It's just that weight makes the blood pressure go up. Any weight."

That seemed to ease her feelings, and we proceeded with the exam. Afterward, I was in the hallway, out of the patient's eyesight. She was on one side of the counter as Margaret, our secretary, was sitting before the new computer on the other side. The waiting room was empty.

Margaret asked, "Insurance?"

"Don't have none," the lady replied.

"Well, then, that will be twenty dollars for today."

With that, the woman overturns her handbag and retrieves some loose change.

That does it!

I couldn't stand idly by. I emerged from the hallway and came to the counter. Picking up the change, I gave it back to the old woman.

"No charge. Today is opening day."

After the lady had gone, Margaret turned to me and said, "You can't make everyone a 'no charge.'"

"I know. But today *is* special."

"What do you want me to do to other patients? Not bill them?"

"No, do what you have to do."

"Bill, everybody?"

"Not if they're like that little old lady."

I tried to laugh, but it was forced.

As I walked away, I thought, *Maybe I should find another line of work.* Followed by, *The old lady probably planned the whole thing, and I fell for it.*

After that, everything went well. It was a gala opening.

Then we learned Margaret had lied on her application.

"We can't have this," Tom said. "What will our patients think if one of them finds out? We have to fire her."

"We?'

"Well, you, really. Of the two of us, you have some experience. Will you do it?"

Thinking of Charlie I replied, "I guess so. There's no one else I can pass the buck to."

The real world is not so funny.

It was a dreary day. After all the patients had gone, I called, "Margaret, can you come here?"

Have to do this, I thought as I took a deep breath. *Might as well get it over with. This boss stuff is not for me.*

After she had sat across from my desk, I asked. "Who are you? You're not Margaret O'Malley."

Realizing we had caught her, she told the truth. "My name is Nadine Farr."

"Why did you lie?"

"Because if I told you the truth, you wouldn't have hired me, and I needed the job."

"Why wouldn't I have hired you? What did you do?"

"I spent some time in prison."

"For what?"

"Embezzling."

"*What?*"

"Office managing is all I know. The temptation to cook the books was too great."

My head was swimming. She was right. We wouldn't have hired her if we knew. But pretending to be someone else was not the answer.

"You're gonna fire me, ain't ya?"

I nodded my head.

With that, she rose and left the room. I lowered my head.

Definitely am suited for the ER. But it can't be Mercy anymore.

My cousin, Lena, temporarily took Nadine/Margaret's place until we could find someone permanent. Then Nancy Eckert's, the ER nurse, sister, Donna, became available, so we hired her.

"Do EKGs, spirometry, and sigmoidoscopy on everyone," Tom advised one afternoon when we were both off from the ER. "They all need them, and Medicare will pay. They take less time than a full exam and pay more."

"But I can't do procedures for procedures' sake," I flashed back.

"Think of it as overhead We don't get paid if we don't put the right code numbers down, and we go under. Then everybody suffers."

If only I could find a little hole and crawl in, so no one sees me. Medicine is not a business! I never had to worry about money before. The ER is looking better all the time.

47

THE FIRE

The year was 1989. The Berlin Wall came down, and I was still working in Mercy's ER in Scranton with a family practice on the side. I smoked and tried many times to quit. It didn't help when a family practitioner who asked his patients to stop for their health smoked himself.

What an example I am!

One weekend, Bob Eckert and I put a stereo in my Chevette. The speakers were in the doors. Without telling me, he ran the wires over the ashtray and through the glove compartment.

On Monday, after working the day shift in the ER, I drove toward the office in nearby Olyphant. I was caught in a traffic jam, so I lit a cigarette while waiting. I had broken the driver's window so it wouldn't move, so I rolled down the passenger's to let the smoke escape.

The ashtray was typically full when I went to snuff out the cancer stick. But I put the cigarette in any way. It started to smoke.

If I just shut the ashtray, no oxygen can fuel the flame.

The ashtray was near the opened window. The wires from the stereo caught fire. In a moment, flames shot out of the glove compartment.

What's going on?

I kicked the dashboard. I don't know why. The fire didn't go out.

This is dangerous! I'm stuck in traffic with a driver's window that won't crank. Now, my car's on fire! Have to get off this road.

I pulled onto an empty side street where a new development was under construction.

Good! No people.

At the end of the road, I spied a bucket turned on its side. I parked the Chevette in the middle of the empty street. Leaving the car, I scrambled for the bucket. Grabbing it, I noticed one of the new houses had an outside faucet. So, I filled the pail with water.

A man's head poked out of the house above me as it was filling. "What are you doing?"

I pointed to the car.

"Go ahead!"

I ran back with the sloshing water to find a bunch of kids around the auto.

*Are they playing Ring-around-the-Rosie? Where did **they** come from? This is just great! The tires will explode. The valves will kill the kids! What a headline! I can see it now. "Smoking Doctor Kills Kids!"*

I herded them away from the car.

When I returned, the inside of the Chevette was all smoke. Everything burned: x-rays, bowling ball, driver's seat. I don't think Chevrolet installs anything unless it is flammable. There must be some tests. My mess added fuel to the flames.

The fire engine arrived after it, too, was caught in the traffic jam.

"Thanks for stopping," the firemen said.

"Stopping! It's *my* car!"

I guess they cannot believe that doctors drive other vehicles besides Mercedes. The firefighters doused the conflagration with water, extinguishing it.

The Chevette was totaled, so I rode to work on the back of the fire truck. Who knows what the patients thought when I dismounted?

When I was safely in the office, Donna called Edie. Later I learned from Donna the conversation went something like this.

"Hello. Dr. Thek is normal," Donna began.

There was a brief pause, and then Edie responded. "He's never been normal. What happened?"

LENA LOANED ME HER CAR—ALSO a Chevette. They must run in the family.

She still has studded snow tires on.

The day after the fire, I drove it home from the office. A cop pulled me over two towns away from where it happened.

"License and registration," he commanded after I had rolled down the window and he had walked to my car. The policeman looked at me through his reflective sunglasses.

"What was I pulled over for?"

"Speeding."

Speeding! Uh-oh. I thought he was gonna warn me about the studded snow tires. I'm in for it now.

"You're not gonna believe this," I started.

He lowered his sunglasses. I could see by his beady eyes this cop was no one with whom to fool.

"Try me," the cop said authoritatively.

"A car fire destroyed my license yesterday."

After a brief pause, he asked, "Are you, Dr. Thek?"

I had purposely avoided giving my name. "Why, yes, as a matter of fact, I am. How did you know?" The policeman started to laugh. I could take many things, but being ridiculed by a cop was not one of them.

"Please, give me a ticket or something," I begged.

He roared.

"Give me a *#*# ticket!"

The policeman laughed hysterically.

"'All I wanted was a Bud Light,' Torch," he replied.

I couldn't understand what was happening. *Why won't he ticket me?*

It turned out the cop was the husband of the fire engine dispatcher and knew all about the fire.

I went to the ER the next night,

"Hello, 'Torch,'" Jean Marie said.

That does it! If the Berlin Wall can come down, I can quit smoking.

Soon after that, I decided an office was not for me either. I was happy in the ER, where nobody paid me for the services rendered except the hospital. I didn't know, and I didn't care from where the money came. I was ignorant and apathetic.

Can care for people without worrying about overhead.

The cost never concerned me. The ER was made for people like me, but I couldn't be in Scranton anymore. It had to be someplace else where I wasn't the boss.

During that time, I wrestled with the idea of The First Principle—GOD or no GOD. I didn't see HIM in my work. Scales must have covered my eyes. I tried, unsuccessfully, to reconcile evolution with the Bible. We can't do it. Many say the Bible is relative, and GOD's day may be a billion years, not twenty-four hours. That was a satisfactory answer to me, then. However, kicking the can down the road doesn't answer anything. That still meant a Creator. I tried not to think about it, but the question gnawed away. It irritated like a grain of sand with an oyster. My pearl was yet to evolve.

48

MOVING ON

That next year was one of the unexpected. In February 1990, John, Suellen's husband, developed an aneurysm in his aortic plastic graft. He had open-heart surgery, but it was too late, and he passed on.

I called Pat McCarthy.

"John died," I mumbled.

"Your brother?"

"No, it's only my brother-in-law."

Only?

I lost it and cried.

What did I say? His boys, Kevin and Mark, are grown. But what about Suellen? Things can never be the same.

On the day of the funeral, it was a cold and wintery day, but clear. During the funeral visitation, Dad called John "son number four." He was.

Memories of the unfinished kitchen floor and the hutch[1] we had worked on together invaded my mind. We laughed at each other's mistakes and slapped each other's backs when things went wrong. And how Suellen bragged about him.

She was right. John was a good man.

Funerals are so depressing for the lost. And, at that moment, I was lost and didn't know it.

What is Suellen gonna do now? Get re-married? At twenty-eight, probably. At thirty-eight, maybe. At forty-eight, I don't think so. She's a widow and will always be one. We all have to do what we can for her. That's what family means.

At the time, I thought: *Dead is gone, from nothing to nothing. Where's the hope in that?*

Now, I am looking forward to seeing him again. I'm sure my sister was, too. He came to understand that we are all sinners saved by grace.[2]

A belief in the reality of Heaven helps. At least then, believers have comfort in thinking that they'll be reunited. That there's something more. Maybe there's something to it. I've straddled the fence long enough. I'm sick of going to funerals.

But how could HE have let this happen if there was a GOD?

ONE NIGHT THAT SUMMER, my brother, Johnny, was visiting Pompton Plains from Japan as usual. His wife of four years, Yoko, stayed behind. Yes, it was John and Yoko. How many people in the world have a brother named Johnny married to a woman named Yoko? I should be an honorary *Beatle.*

I wondered, *will they ever put their names on the mailbox? Hoodlums have firebombed his cars twice already. Better not!*

He was accustomed to saying there were three good things about teaching— June, July, and August. Now he could add a fourth, and her name is Yoko.

I frequently visited my father and mother alone on the way to see my literary agent in Fort Lee. I enjoyed the leisurely drive and found playing tapes during the two hours restful.

Johnny and I were sleeping upstairs at Mom and Dad's home. The radio awakened me.

"Why are you getting up?" he asked sleepily from his bed across the room.

"I think someone left the radio on. I'm going downstairs to shut it off."

I hurriedly dressed and went down the steps toward the noise. It was the radio in the dining room, all right. There was my *mother* with her ear up against it.

"What are you doing? It's two o'clock in the morning!" I exclaimed.

"Shh! I'm listening to the ninth inning of the Mets game in California."

For once, I was speechless. My father, I could almost see, but my *mother*. It boggled my wee mind. What kind of a chance did I have of growing up normally in a home filled with Mets fanatics? Most people settled differences of opinion by referring to the Bible. Not us! We used the Baseball Encyclopedia. We used stats like rapiers.

THE SAME SUMMER, the boys, Mike, and I traveled to Maine to climb Mt. Katadhin. The topographical chart showed two possible trails.

This one looks shorter on the map.

It was shorter, all right, but more perpendicular.

Upon reaching the top, we found it was the wrong mountain! It was Mt. Pamola. I already had a "P'" for Pikes Peak and still needed a "K" for the AHA[3].

Now, who goes to Maine and climbs the wrong mountain?

"We can still make it," I said, looking at the map. "All we have to do is climb along the Knife's Edge and Chimney Peaks to get to Katadhin."

The peak loomed on the horizon. The trail looked good on the map. Was the mountain laughing?

Josh and Mike had no trouble with the boulders and cliffs, but Jeremiah and I were another story.

"Dad, I can't do it," he said finally.

I was secretly glad. I couldn't go on without him. I turned and looked at the peak, *Katahdin, you and I have unfinished business.*

Was I stupid or what?

Josh and Mike stopped climbing to rejoin us.

I studied the map again.

"We can go down this way," I said while pointing at a trail. We reversed but the descent was more difficult than the ascent. It was the descent of Half Dome all over again.

Don't I ever learn?

"Isn't–that an–eagle?" I said, pointing skyward toward a swooping bird while catching my breath.

We heard a familiar "Caw-caw-caw."

"Dad, it's only a crow," Jeremiah enlightened me.

We all want to be eagles in our hearts but wind up being crows. GOD loves us anyway.[4]

We were exhausted when we reached the bottom. We had driven all that way and accomplished nothing. After we slept all night, we drove the next day back to New Jersey and Mays Landing, where Lena lived, stopping to drop off Mike. Inside their condo, I said to Kathryn, "I saw some Wild Kathryns."

"Some what?"

"Wild Kathryns."

"And what are they?"

"Pregnant moose."

She looked at me askance and contorted her lips. "Oh, Uncle Joe."

No wonder she didn't believe me. The previous year I took the boys up to Mt. Marcy.

"Watch out for the Maya-Maya bugs," I warned them in a severe tone.

"The what?" Mike asked.

"Maya-Maya bugs. Their bite is deadly, and they look like ordinary bumblebees. So, watch out."

He continually looked over his shoulder for them in our ascent up the mountain.

When we returned to their condo, I told Kathryn, "We made it to the top despite the deadly Maya-Maya bugs."

"Oh, Uncle Joe, there's no such thing."

"Give me the dictionary, and I'll prove it to you."

She handed me the dictionary and, without Kathryn being able to see, I looked up the tsetse fly. Still hiding it, I read, "Any of several bloodsucking American bugs of the genus *Glossina*, often carrying and transmitting pathogenic trypanosomes to human beings and livestock." I changed "African" to "American" and "flies" to "bugs." Keeping "Glossina" convinced her. Children are so easy to fool.

Satan must have a field day with us. We'll believe almost anything: The Big Bang Theory, The Theory of Relativity, Evolution, and all because we don't believe the truth about GOD. It's sad. I don't have all the answers. I don't even know all the questions! All I can see for sure is what has happened to me.

∾

A COUPLE of weeks after the Katahdin hike, I received a call from Dr. Frank Schneider, ER director of Wilkes-Barre General.

"Do you want to moonlight down here? Kind of check us out."

Why not? I'm unhappy at Mercy. Poor management has everybody jumping ship.

"Okay."

When a full-time position opportunity arose, Frank offered it to me and sweetened the offer by asking me to be the Assistant Director working only nights. I liked working there, so I accepted.

I enjoyed the eight nights on and six off schedule and was second in command after Frank, Wilkes-Barre General's ER saw some trauma cases too. The job was perfect for me.

Wilkes-Barre had better working conditions. Eventually, I reversed roles by taking a moonlighting position at Mercy. I was still loyal to Mercy with all its warts. After eight years, deciding to go wasn't easy.

My kids have grown up while I was there! But I know I have to move on.

They had their own ER department. The x-ray suite was down the hall; a nurses' aide was on every shift, and a desk secretary was located in the back, with receptionists in the front foyer. Security was right next-door and where psychiatric patients waited to be evaluated. It was truly a city ER with trauma included.

Some place I can really use my skills.

I worked full-time at Wilkes-Barre General starting in January. By Valentine's Day, I was sure I had made the right choice.

By spring, I was optimistic about Wilkes-Barre General. I could see my life improving. Then the walls caved in.

49

VAL AGAIN

Val reappeared in 1989. She visited my parents' house. They weren't home, so Val left a message next door to them. "Call me" was scribbled along with her number and address. The neighbor gave it to my mother, and she brought it to me. Temptation came on its own.

What should I do? Tell her to get lost? I'm married now. But she lives in North Carolina. That's far away. What could go wrong?

As I said, I was (am) stupid.

I only needed a little nudge. An evil voice inside me kept saying, *You took a vow to 'go steady.' Isn't that like marriage?*

You can say I wasn't responsible because I was only a kid. But I still *felt* responsible. I have always carried the conviction that any vow is serious. I possessed a strong conviction one's word was his bond and a measure of manhood. Years later, I learned that the Bible advises us not to break an oath if one is taken at all. [1]

Satan will use anything to get a foothold. I knew better, but Edie was in school. Our marriage wasn't perfect by any means.

Know what I'll do. Send her a letter. What could go wrong? It's just a letter wondering how she's doing.

So, I sent a letter to Valerie. I went to the mailbox daily, hoping that Edie hadn't been there first.

Why is my heart racing?

Valerie eventually answered my letter. I stopped and almost phoned her secretly on the way back from Bill's. I even went so far as to enter a phone booth, but an unreasonable sense of guilt was too strong.

This is crazy!

I returned to the car and drove home.

It wasn't long before I received another letter from Val. The words were innocent enough, but I couldn't shake the nagging worry Edie would find out and bust the bubble I was riding.

Can't go on like this. Have to tell her. She should hear it from me. It's all so—so—innocent.

I sat with Edie in the dining room after shutting the door to avoid the kids' earshot. "This must be serious," she said.

"It is."

Her demeanor changed to one of expectation.

"Well, what is it now?"

Is this a good idea? Too late now. Best thing is to jump in the water.

"I've been writing letters back and forth to Val for six months," I confessed. "Nothing more." I neglected to add "Yet."

Edie was dumbfounded.

"Valerie? From high school?"

"Yes."

Then she started to cry. That was a woman's weapon against a man. Edie, however, seldom used it. Her tears were real and they cut me.

"Why are you doing that?" I asked.

She wiped away the tears, thought for a moment, then said, "Think of what you have done."

"I haven't done anything!"

"Yes, you have. Think about it."

Then she kissed me on the cheek and left the room.

How can I love both of them? Isn't love exclusive?

I had never gotten Val out of my system—first love was tenacious.

And yet, I cared deeply for Edie—the mother of my children. It confused me.

Edie won't understand about Val. She'd see her as a competitor. Can't just drown my troubles in work. That's falling apart, too. Can't talk to the kids. They're way too young. Besides, they'd never understand. Not sure I do. Aren't I supposed to set a good example? All I've done is betray Edie and Val is far away in North Carolina. I'm trapped, and I don't see a way out.

I learned that Val lived with her son and daughter near her mother. Life is ironic. The mother she didn't get along with was living close by. I laughed to myself.

Figures.

Val had a good job at IBM. She divorced her first husband and never mentioned a second or Bill Hurley, either.

I did not see Val, but we kept writing. Then, I received a phone call at work. The nurse handed me the phone without me knowing who it was.

"Hello? Doctor Thek here."

"This is Val," she said in the sexiest voice I'd ever heard.

I was speechless. She had caught me off guard. My pulse quickened, and my stomach lurched while I searched for something clever to say. I was ecstatic as a schoolboy again.

"Ain't ya' gonna say something? "she finally asked.

I couldn't think, so I lied. "You surprised me, is all. We're swamped here. Can I call you back?"

She accepted that and hung up.

Now, what am I gonna do? I wondered. *Have to call her. What will I say? Wonder what this is about?*

The evil voice advised, *Just be yourself.* The good voice said, *Danger. Tell her you're happily married.*

Don't listen to HIM, the bad voice continued. *HE doesn't know what HE's talking about. It's only a phone call.*

To my shame, I listened to the wrong voice.

Was I stupid or what? Again, Satan wormed his way into my life. It's easy blaming Satan, but the truth is I was responsible, too. I was in an abandoned doorway, waiting for him to weave his web of lies. We are all sinners saved by grace.[2] Thank GOD for HIS grace.

I called the next day, making sure I was alone.

"Hi, it's me. What's up? And don't say the sky, or I'll hang up."

We exchanged pleasantries and got caught up on a bit of history. I did most of the talking. Once I felt at ease, I rambled on. Hearing her voice again was refreshing.

She's an oasis in this desert that surrounds me, I reasoned.

"Things at home are crazy," I admitted. The letters had loosened my tongue, not that it needed much loosening. "Between raising the kids, satisfying Edie, and my work, I never know which end is up. Jeremiah is always in detention for something, and we face the real possibility of him not finishing high school. My relationship with Edie is murky. I'm tired of hearing about women's lib and who will pick up the kids. Family life is getting me down. I count the weekends until retirement. Nothing seems to be going right."

"When you say you have trouble, "satisfying Edie," do you mean sexually?" she asked.

"No, no, no. It has nothing to do with that. I'm talking about everyday things like the color of the carpet or things you wear."

"Color of the carpet?"

"I know it sounds silly, but once she wanted to change the carpet because of its color."

"Oh, poor baby."

"Who? Me or her?"

"Both."

We became silent for a moment, before finally Val said, "I have to tell you why I called."

"I was wondering that myself."

"Next month, I'm traveling to New York State to sell computer programs. But I need someone to pick me up at the airport. I'm flying into Stewart. Can you do it?"

The voices went to battle. *It's only a ride,* one said. *But where will it lead?* The other said. *I need a release,* I rationalized.

I decided to throw caution away.

"Yes, I can do it," I replied.

I began planning a harmless interlude.

I can pick her up when she lands. Any friend would at least do that.

The weeks passed slowly. Finally, the day of her arrival came. Edie was away with the kids in Philadelphia.

Perfect! No one will ever know!

I met Val at Stewart airport in upstate New York. She hadn't changed much. If anything, she was more beautiful than ever. I would recognize that graceful walk anywhere.

"Good of you to pick me up," she said after we'd exchanged pleasantries.

"I wasn't doing anything today, anyway."

"Well, now you are."

What's that supposed to mean?

We got in the car and drove across the Hudson River to Danbury, Connecticut.

"I love you," she said after we had reminisced in the car for a half hour.

Her admission took me aback. Memories of losing my virginity flooded my mind. "I-I love you too," I stammered.

Am I in a dream? All the different roads I've traveled lead here.

Old Satan had me nodding my head in agreement.

I took Val to her room at the Holiday Inn before we went out for some beer. Alcohol and old flames don't mix.

"I had a second husband, a historian," Val said with speech slightly slurred as we relaxed in chairs back in her room. We were alone, right where I wanted to be.

She got up, kicked off her shoes, and plopped on the bed. "I don't know why I married him. Maybe I thought he was you."

After a couple of uncomfortable moments of silence, Val patted the space beside her on the bed.

"I don't bite," she said,

Open to temptation, I left my chair, removed my sneakers, and joined her on the bed.

"And then there was Bill," she continued taking another sip of beer.

"Bill? Who is he?"

"Bill Hurley. He was great with Matt in North Carolina. I got pregnant by him when I was on The Pill."

"How did you get pregnant?"

"You being a doctor, I thought you'd know," Val laughed. "Seriously, I was a therapeutic failure. So, I had to get an abortion, didn't I? Then they gave me Catholic birth control—a hysterectomy. All I wanted was a blue-eyed baby. Now I can't have any."

None of this would've happened if I'd been around.

"All I wanted was a blue-eyed baby," she repeated.

I was stunned. I felt sorry for her, for me, for everybody. Through my tears, I thought I saw everything I ever wanted or dreamed about lying beside me.

She sat up and kissed me gently on the lips. Before I knew it, I was kissing her hard. We almost tore each other's clothes off. Maybe I should have resisted temptation, but I didn't. I broke the Seventh Commandment.[3]

Was it worth it? Definitely not, for I betrayed Edie again, the best woman I had ever known until then. She's not perfect, but, hey, neither am I. We shattered my kids' lives. GOD hates divorce[4]. My actions are inexcusable. I am a sinner in need of redemption like everyone else.

Afterward, I drove to my parent's place in New Jersey, where Johnny was visiting.

"I got caught in a traffic jam." I broke another commandment. I lied.[5]

I also learned my Uncle Pete passed away that night, and I still had Val's scent about me.

What am I gonna do?

50

THE ADVENTURE

Val and Katahdin were both mountains of unfinished business for me. The summer of 1991 provided an opportunity for me to finalize both.

Josh would start at Drexel in the fall. Therefore, I decided to tackle Katahdin first while I had time and money.

I called Bob Eckert and asked, "Want to climb Mt. Katahdin?"

"Mt. what?"

"Katahdin. In Maine. It's where the Appalachian Trail starts."

"The what?"

"Never mind. We need a 'K' for the AHA," I answered, fidgeting with my hands.

"Don't start that again."

"Well, are you in or not?"

There was silence for a few moments, and then Bob answered, "I do need a vacation. The kids are making me pull my hair out. When are we talking?"

"Next Tuesday through Friday."

"Next week? Nothing like leaving things for the last minute.

"Is that a 'Yes'?"

"Who else is going?"

"So far, it's just us two. I'll call Bill Ranetsky and see what he says."

"Who's he?'

"A friend. You and him will get along,"

Bob groaned and then said, "Well, okay."

Don't do me any favors, I thought as I hung up and called Bill.

He was the polar opposite. Bill was his effervescent self, especially after I mentioned climbing Katadhin.

"Is that a big mountain?" he asked, but his tone was one of eagerness.

"The biggest in Maine. Rocky. Steep. But it's only a little over 5400 feet. But because it's so far north, it's way above timberline."

"Count me in."

On top of Mt. Katadhin

I cradled the receiver feeling proud of myself for having talked my two buddies into going. My satisfaction didn't last long.

Val called me at work the next day.

"Have a few days off. Can fly up there next Friday," she said excitedly.

"I'll be there," I replied, my hormones thinking. After I'd hung up, I realized what I'd done.

Now, what do I do? I've double-booked. Can't tell Bob because he might tell Nancy[1], and she'll tell Edie.

Oh, the webs we weave.

I called Bob first. "Look, I have to move the trip up a day," I said.

"Why?"

I was caught off-guard. "I have to be back by Thursday," I replied honestly enough.

"Why?"

Knowing he was a Mel Brooks[2] fan, I said, "Look, I didn't 'expect the Inquisition.'" Bob laughed, and I continued, "Can you make it?"

"Sure. Wasn't doing nothing on Monday anyway."

"Now you are."

I hung up and called Bill. I used a different tactic—the truth.

"*#*# her brains out," he advised.

"Don't tell Bob. Tell him I have to get back for Josh's orientation if he asks."

However, I don't make a good liar. Bob took one look at me the morning we left for Maine, and I confessed.

"Why you, sly dog," he said.

"Just don't tell Nancy."

"My lips are sealed," and Bob made a motion as if he was locking his lips and throwing away the key.

Neither of them ever advised me to break off my fling with Val. But to be honest, I wouldn't have listened if they had.

We could climb Katadhin on Tuesday, Wednesday we'd sight-see, Thursday we'd travel, and I'd be back to meet Val on Friday. After seeing her, I would drive to Philadelphia to attend Josh's orientation with Edie. I forgot one little thing—my conscience. Lust does that—clogs the intellect.

What a trip! Call it Billy-Bob-Joe's Great Adventure.

We drove to Katadhin through the night. I suffered from a cold, but we were to hike to the top the next day. Oh, to be young again! On second thought, that's probably not a good idea.

We hiked through the forest along a trail that was not so difficult.

"This ain't so hard," a cocky Bill said.

But it was long. When we finally emerged from the woods, there was a lake shrouded by Katadhin behind it. Katadhin loomed before us as its shadow was cast for miles.

I looked at its imposing rock façade and wondered, *Can we make it?*

It looked different from this vantage point. I almost wished we had taken the wrong trail like before.

Bob said, "We're going up there?"

"What's the matter? You scared?" I asked.

"You bet I am. I'm not stupid. How are we gonna do it?"

"One foot in front of the other."

"Very funny."

"No, I mean it. Don't look up or down. Just look at where you are and go. Before you know it, we'll be at the top."

"Sure," a skeptical Bob answered.

At any rate, we started up. It was a strenuous hike, almost straight up at points and very rocky. About halfway up, Bob lost his footing and somersaulted. He came down with a pyramidal rock between his legs.

"Wow! If–I'd–have–gone–an–inch–in–any–direction, I–would–have–been–castrated," he said breathlessly. "That–was–close. Whose–idea–was–this–anyway?"

They both looked at me, and I had nowhere to hide.

There was an elderly gentleman on the trail. He puffed, "You–couldn't–pay–me–to–do–this–torture, and–we–do–it–for–free!"

As I'd said, we continued with one foot in front of the other. One step became two, five, a hundred, then thousands. Time seemed stuck as onward and upward we slowly trudged.

We finally reached the top and looked down to see the lake below with the wooded valley through which we had hiked. All thought of the climb was erased from our memory as the view at the top was unlike any other, I'd seen in the East. We were way above the timberline. Our view was unimpeded. Katahdin was more like the Rockies and steep. We'd already forgotten how difficult it was to climb. We were like new mothers who forget the labor pains as soon as the babies are born.

Bob was delighted, and was a different person.

"Wow! What a view! Nancy and the kids will never believe that I climbed this. C'mon, take a picture of me at the top."

And that's what we did. There was a big sign announcing the height and the start of the Appalachian Trail. We draped around it and went out on a rocky ledge to look down, ensuring we took a picture. Who cared if it was dangerous? It was a photo op.

Going down was a lot easier. Now we had gravity working in our favor. We stopped before entering the forest and took a final, prideful look back.

Under the trees with no view, our thoughts turned naturally to dinner.

"On the way into town, I saw a Chinese restaurant," Bill said.

"Sounds good. Let's go," I agreed.

After we were seated, Bill requested, "Chopsticks, please."

"What are they?" the waitress replied in her Maine accent.

Bill rolled his eyes. "This is a Chinese restaurant. I want some chopsticks."

The American waitress replied, "I've never heard of 'em."

"I demand chopsticks!" Bill roared.

"Just hold your horses," I intervened. "Can't you eat rice with a spoon just this once?"

"Well—"

"Pretty please."

"Okay."

In Bill's defense, what kind of Oriental restaurant has never heard of chopsticks? On the other hand, it was the middle of Maine.

The next day, we booked a cottage outside Bar Harbor, then explored Cadillac Mountain and Acadia National Park in the morning. You can drive to the top of Cadillac to be at the highest point on the east coast and see the point where the sun first appears on that coast every morning.

Back in the town of Bar Harbor, there was a floating restaurant. We got on board.

As we were seated, I asked our waitress, "Where is the menu?"

"There ain't none," the waitress answered with a Maine twang.

I rose to leave.

"We have a menu," the bartender interjected.

All of us sat down to peruse it. Everything on the menu looked good.

"I'll have the lobster with shrimp cocktail as an appetizer," I said as my mouth watered.

The waitress answered, "That's the dinner menu. Lunch is bein' served now."

"Where's the lunch menu?"

"Like I said, there ain't none."

We ate our light lunch and returned to the cottage where we slept. On Thursday morning, my friends and I started home. A few hours into our trip back, with Maine and New Hampshire behind us, Bill had just taken the wheel while I was in the back. Bob was in the passenger seat with the map.

"Say, why don't we take in Fenway?" I suggested.

"What's that?" Bob asked.

"Where the Red Sox play. It's on our way."

With that, Bob, as navigator, looked at a map. "That's way out of the way."

"Including the game, only a few hours."

"Excuse me, but weren't you in a hurry to get back?"

"Got it all figured out. We'll be back tonight. No problem. One doesn't come up here and not see Fenway."

Bob rolled his eyes.

"We need a break anyway," Bill said, taking the exit for Boston.

I had been there once before but hadn't gone in because the umpires, led by Ron Luciano[3],had gone on strike and formed a picket line. With my history, I couldn't cross it. That had been years before, and I had yet to go inside. Fenway was a shrine that any true baseball fan could not avoid.

Bill was driving and became lost in Boston. He sped up as if we would get there sooner.

"You're driving like you're in an ambulance!" I shouted. "Can't we just stop and get directions? You have no idea where you're going!"

He continued darting and dodging through traffic.

"Where's the fire?" I asked.

Finally, we pulled over for directions. Bill acted like asking for them was beneath him. With the instructions, we finally made it to Fenway. We even found our seats. That's two for two. But we were behind a pole. Seeing the game was challenging. Foul ball! But, we're in Fenway! Then I realized the oppressive heat. *Holy cow, it's hot!*

That night we returned, arriving late Thursday night in Pennsylvania. My buddies wished me luck with Val. Edie was already in Philadelphia visiting with her parents—both good people.

Fenway Park, Boston.

51

THE SECOND TIME

The next day, I dropped Bill in Reading, then drove to the airport outside Scranton to pick up Val. She disembarked the plane in her tight-fitting jean shorts and blue cotton blouse. Her long legs fairly screamed sex.

"Hi!" she yelled, waving enthusiastically to me as she emerged from the long exit ramp. I immediately put my finger to my lips. I didn't want to draw attention to us. Val pouted.

We hurried off to my car. I was nervous, thinking that someone I knew might see us. I tried not to look at her legs until we were safely in the car. Then she leaned over and kissed me on the lips.

"Not here," I rasped. "Someone will see!"

Val backed away. She pouted again

We drove on Route 81 east, out of Scranton. I relaxed the farther we went, finally stopping for dinner at a Mexican restaurant near High Point[1]. I drove that far (about sixty miles) to be sure no one recognized me. The first encounter with our making love had been spontaneous. At least, it was on my part. We planned the second.

After we sat, Val ordered Spanish Fly to drink. "I hear it makes you sexy," she said.

"Believe me. You don't need an aphrodisiac."

"A what?"

"Aphrodisiac."

"What's that?"

"A sex stimulant."

Oh," she giggled. "But I still don't see what that has to do with a hair-do."

"Who said anything about a hair-do?'

"Didn't you just say it begins with an Afro?"

I looked at her askance, but she was serious. Our waiter appeared and asked, "What will you have?"

"The *El Diablo*[2]," I ordered.

It was appropriately named. The devil was tempting me that night.

The waiter returned shortly with the steaming fish extravaganza. While my mouth feasted on *El Diablo*, my eyes settled on her.

She's beautiful. How do I deserve this?

We returned to the motel in the shadow of High Point near the Delaware River on the Pennsylvania side. We looked for a moment at the obelisk that presides over the valley.

"Kinda makes me think of what's coming up," she said.

I couldn't stand it any longer. We kissed and hurriedly took the elevator to our room. Safely inside, our clothes came off as we toppled onto the bed.

Afterward, both of us reached for a cigarette.

I'm a sinner like everybody else. I did it.

Then the turmoil hit.

How did I get myself into this mess? I never wanted to hurt anyone, but again I've betrayed the best woman I've ever known!

I tried to convince myself that there was no First Principle, but something started it all. My logic couldn't deny it, and I found I could not abandon a First Cause.

When I drove her back to the airport, she tried to hold my hand after exiting the car. I withdrew it, "We have to be discreet."

Isn't that what I've been for over twenty years? Isn't my marriage to Edie a farce when I'd always been in love with Val? But I do love Edie, too. Oh, what have I done?

"Don't look back when I board the plane," Val ordered.

Reminds me of *Casablanca*. Maybe I should have because I would never see her again.

52

THE DIVORCE

I continued to Philadelphia, where I joined Edie at Josh's orientation. After the program, we joined other parents and toured the campus grounds. We ate dinner and then left the group for a quiet walk back to the dorm room reserved for us. There was no TV and little else to do, so we snuggled in bed.

Have to tell her. Could I have picked up something?

"I slept with Val," I admitted while holding her close.

At first, she was silent, then pushed me away, screaming, "HOW COULD YOU?"

Why did I admit it? Was it for her or me? If only I could find a hole to crawl in.

"I've given you everything!" Edie insisted angrily.

"No, you didn't! You're going to school and preparing to leave me!"

"*Are you nuts?* I'm doing all this for *us*—the family!"

I felt the tension in the room. We had been angry at each other before, but not like this. It was like a bomb exploded in our room. I'm still breathing the fallout.

"Men!" she scoffed. "What is it with you anyway?"

"Women are not perfect either!"

"But it's a man's world! We change our names to yours. We get half the pay for the same job—"

"Oh, here we go again."

"Well, it's the truth. Now, this."

Edie became silent again as the door of her mind slammed shut. The atmosphere was meat-locker cold.

"I'll sleep on the floor," I said, thinking the marriage was over. I was wrong, for a little while anyway. We hadn't inflicted enough pain yet.

THE PHONE RANG at work a few days later, interrupting a slow night. Bob Burke, the head night nurse, answered.

"ER," he replied gruffly. Cupping his hands over the receiver, he whispered. "It's for you."

Now, who would call at this hour of night? Must be bad news.

"Hello?" I answered hesitantly.

"This is Val," a sexy voice replied.

My heart pounded.

"Where are you?" I asked, not knowing what else to say.

"In North Carolina."

"I thought you might be here."

"I'm not, but I can see you in New York City next month."

"Great! I can visit Pat McCarthy before I see you."

On my way home from working nights at Wilkes-Barre General, I'd stop and call Val from a phone booth. When I got home, Edie always knew I had because I was late. Edie was understandably cool to me. I couldn't wait to go to Pat Mullin's apartment to get away. Finally, the day arrived. We drove to a gym he owned where he practiced karate. While he did, I called Val, "I can't wait to see you."

There was silence on the other end.

"Hello? Are you there?"

"Yes, I'm here," Val answered. "Bill wants me back."

Oh great! Ruin my marriage, then go to Bill! He's in North Carolina and single, while I'm in Pennsylvania and married. I can't compete, and I don't want to.

But in my heart, I knew it wasn't all her fault. I played a willing part. *I'm so-o guilty.*

After several months of my sleeping on the floor and walking on eggshells to avoid each other, we put our differences aside and became husband and wife again. But both feared the solution couldn't last. We agreed to see a marriage counselor.

The first couple of counseling sessions went well. However, at one point, I admitted, "I slept with Val twice."

"Twice! I only know about once," Edie said testily.

"Now, let's not lose control," the counselor advised. "You should get away together and get to know each other again."

Edie and I spent a weekend in the Poconos[1] together. Both of us tried, but something was missing. It takes years to build a trusting relationship with a person. It is destroyed in one moment of weakness and stupidity.

All this aggravation and guilt? For what? A roll in the hay? But a man who understood real love wouldn't have done it, would he?

Our marriage was cold all through the winter into the summer of 1992. Edie and I were still trying to reconcile, but we had changed. We didn't talk for fun anymore.

In the autumn I went with Bob and Bill to the Adirondacks as a chance to escape for a while. My pals and I visited the Ausable Chasm and then hiked Mount Algonquin for an "A^2."

As usual, after a hike, Bob and Bill phoned their wives.

Why don't I feel like calling Edie? I should.

The conflict stirred in me *en route* to our Chinese restaurant.

"I have something for you," I said to Bill before dinner.

"What?" he asked excitedly.

"Congratulations! You've won the Golden Chopsticks Award!" I said, handing him chopsticks I had painted gold and brought along.

"Thank you," he laughed.

∾

I WAS GOING about my business that November when a stray paper in the kitchen caught my attention.

What's this?

I began reading it.

"The Clarks Summit Chronicles by Jeremiah Thek."

Uh-oh. This can't be good news.

"Our *#*#*# English teacher … "

I was beyond angry.

Where does he get language like that?

I picked up the paper and entered the family room, where Jeremiah lounged on the couch. "What's this?" I screamed, throwing the paper at him.

Jeremiah brushed it aside. "Nothin'. Just somethin' I wrote. It's only a copy."

"Copy?" I roared. "You mean there are others?"

He nodded. "Plenty. They're all over school."

"Please don't tell me the teacher knows about this."

"She read it. Said I misspelled some words."

"Why, you little *#*#*#*."

I lost control. Grabbing Jeremiah by the neck, I lifted him off the couch and started to strangle him.

What am I doing?

My hands went limp as I stared at them, releasing him. He fell back on the couch.

Edie came from another room to his rescue.

"And what are *you* doing?" she asked. "I heard you two fighting. Calm down."

"Read this!" I said, gathering the Chronicles from Jeremiah.

"Already have. Teenage stuff."

"Teenage stuff?"

"Hey, don't get mad at me." After a pause, she insisted, "Get your coat."

"My coat? For what?"

"For High Point. It can be cold this time of year."

"High Point? Why?"

"For the sunset. If we leave now, we can see it."

We drove east toward the park. I glanced at Edie.

We've been through a lot together.

I thought of the union, college, medical school, residency, the kids, and work.

Couldn't have done it without her. She truly is my better half. Is it over?

"Thanks," I said.

"For what?

"For being in my life."

At the top of High Point, we sat on our favorite park bench. With no leaves on trees to obstruct our view, we could see out over the Delaware River

"That's strange," I said while pointing downward. "There's two canoes on the river. That's very peculiar at this time of year."

We looked closely. At first, the canoes converged, and then they pulled away.

"What are they doing?" I wondered.

"Probably just crossing the river."

Indeed, the gap between them widened.

I concluded, all good things must come to an end.

"This isn't working," I said to her.

"I know."

We both were silent. There were no tears. We both knew it was over and were relieved it wasn't a scene.

"Perhaps, we should divorce." Who said it? I don't know.

It doesn't matter. To our shame, we both agreed. The two of us needed GOD, but we only had a life-less First Principle. And like Aristotle's First Cause Uncaused, neither one of us was moved or showed any emotion. By going our ways and doing it ourselves, we made mistakes. The children and we suffered. It's the stupidest thing I've ever done and most regretful.

If we stay together, we'll probably fight before the children. Is that better?

I tried to convince myself of that. I loved Edie, but we needed to separate to grow.

Some questions didn't have answers; at least, they weren't readily apparent. A land mine was planted in our marriage, and somehow, I stepped on it. It didn't matter if I planted it myself. It destroyed the trust in our relationship. With the decision made, the antagonism between us evaporated somewhat. Edie taught me how to cook and revealed the house's quirks, so I could keep it clean.

She stayed in school, and her college graduation came in May 1993. I worked the previous night. Because of that, I was sleepy and didn't attend.

"Why didn't you come?" she asked.

"Too tired. No sleep last night."

"I don't believe you. This was very important to me."

"Are you calling me a liar?"

"It was a beautiful ceremony."

"Don't change the subject!"

"You should have been there!"

"Now you can move out! I'm supposed to be happy about that?"

"Supportive is too much to ask?"

"I've got news for you! The world doesn't revolve around Edie!"

Edie moved out. We finalized the divorce the following winter. It was a cold day. She left the kids and the home to my care for two years. Edie moved nearby, and Shannon stayed with her a few years later.

What was the incentive? For both of us, it was our freedom.[3]

I was not a good example, and it negatively impacted the children. Eduardo was right. We should have worked harder on reconciliation. At the time, I thought divorce was the right thing to do. Knowing what I know now, I would have behaved differently and not agreed so readily to it, perhaps not at all.

However, as they say, "It takes two to tango." If either party wants a divorce, the marriage will not work. All the propaganda about feminism doesn't keep anybody warm at night.

Still, wish I had it to do over. Probably jump at the opportunity to be married again—to Edie or someone else. One never knows.

NOTES

Preface

1. 1 Peter 3:15

1. Working and Meeting Dominic

1. Jonah 3:7-10
2. Matthew 3:1 2; Mark 1:15; Luke 13:1-5
3. Exodus 21:24; Leviticus 24:20

2. Funny George and Margot's Place

1. Tuckerman's Ravine – a ravine on the east side ascent of Mount Washington.
2. Aachen, Germany – where my paternal grandfather was born.
3. MCAT – Medical College Admission Test

3. Uncle Ray

1. Deuteronomy 10:18-19; John 19:26-27

4. Mr. Rufallo

1. Aqua regia – a combination of nitric acid and hydrochloric acid

6. Getting into Medical School

1. And I did – *A Question of God's Balance* Volumes 1 and 2

7. Val Again

1. Dawn – Val's younger sister

8. Moving for Medical School

1. Ed Halicki – a pitcher for the San Francisco Giants
2. Mimeograph machine – a copier – you had to put different pages of carbon paper on a round cylinder for each page. It was tedious work.
3. Printer – back then, a printer was a person

9. The Phone Call

1. Passaic Tech – a high school where Johnny taught

10. The Shelter

1. SETA – I don't remember what is stands for.

14. More Medical School

1. Hemothorax – medical term for blood in the chest cavity.
2. Azygous Vein – a big vein that crosses the spine.

15. Jimmy Comes Home

1. Three Mile Island – a meltdown of a nuclear power plant

16. Geisinger

1. At least that's how he tells it, and he swears it's true. However, Dr. Ross could exaggerate a wee bit.
2. Handicapped – each team had five bowlers. You totaled the averages for both teams and gave the lesser team 80% of the difference. E.g., if the difference was 100 pins, then you gave away 80 pins.

19. Life Outside the ER

1. Luke 12:15-21.
2. Harpo Marx – one of the famous Marx brothers
3. Fingertip – a ball that naturally hooks with shortened finger-holes.

20. The Second Year at Geisinger

1. Heparin – an anticoagulant
2. Journey - a famous rock band then
3. Harry Belafonte - a famous Jamaican-American singer who popularized Calypso music.
4. John Africa - Born Vincent Leaphart. Years later, in 1985, the mayor ordered a bomb dropped on the house he occupied. A fire resulted. The entire block (sixty-five homes) went up in flames. The documentary *Let It Burn* is about that incident.

21. The Residents' Union

1. Minimum wage was $3.35 then. With time and a half for overtime, Geisinger should've paid us at least $334/week, not the $270 we were paid.
2. Scut work – menial or dangerous jobs that no one else would do, like starting IVs, drawing blood, etc.
3. James 3:8 - Yes, it is.
4. Jim Taylor – a fullback for the Green Bay Packers in the late '60s
5. At their heart - see 1 Samuel 13:14
6. Foley – a urinary catheter
7. Ma Williams – one of our matronly nurses

22. Bill

1. Penetrating trauma – There were no gunshots or stab wounds. They were confined to the city.
2. Kool and the Gang – an early '80s rock band
3. Dog lab – before doing procedures on humans, we did them on animals like dogs.

23. Practical Jokes

1. Mariel boatlift – From Mariel, Cuba, to Florida. Around 125,000 refugees, many of whom were from prison or psychiatric wards.
2. OCD – Obsessive-Compulsive Disorder
3. Otoscope – a pocket device to look in an ear

24. Soccer Coach

1. Pig Pen – a character in *Peanuts* who always had a dust cloud flying around his feet.

25. Barry the Big Mouth

1. nickel-dime-quarter – a cheap poker game
2. Pot – the money for that hand in the middle of the table
3. Deuteronomy 32:35; Romans 12:19

26. The Conference

1. sensimilla marijuana – seedless and more potent

27. Appendicitis

1. Bigeminy -every other beat was abnormal and could lead to ventricular fibrillation and death.
2. PVCs -Premature Ventricular Contractions can lead to a deadly rhythm.

28. Mercy Hospital

1. $70,000 – To a resident making about $15,000, $70,000 was a lot of money, especially back then.

30. Settling In

1. Galatians 3:28
2. Jed Clampett – iconic TV character played by Buddy Ebson in *The Beverly Hillbillies*11

31. Patrick McCarthy

1. VCR – An obsolete Video Cassette Recorder
2. Gate Night - Mischief Night, the night before Halloween

32. Ian O'Grady

1. Cottage – we called it a "camp."
2. Winterize – drain the pipes, and make the camp secure from critters and people for the winter.

33. Bill Again

1. Eighteenth – the last hole on a golf course
2. Matt. 18:3-4
3. Spike Lee – an actor/producer of the '80s

34. The Highland Avenue House

1. Jim Dandy's – a restaurant
2. Festival of Lights - Hanukkah

37. Disney World

1. Illuminations – The Disney light show

38. Work

1. Mercy Hospital – There were four in PA – all affiliated. Nationwide – Mercy is the second largest hospital organization – behind the VA. I had worked as a resident for a month at the one in Pittsburgh. This Mercy was in Scranton.
2. MICU – pronounced "**Mick**-U"
3. 2 Corinthians 4:18
4. MVA – Motor Vehicle Accident
5. MAST – Military Anti-Shock Trousers. Pneumatic. Designed to increase circulation to the brain and vital organs at the expense of the extremities.
6. CV – Cardio-Vascular
7. Hebrews 9:27
8. EMS – Emergency Medical Systems

39. Day Shift

1. GP – General Practitioner
2. Blowing – enlarging, indicating his brain was dying and herniating
3. ET -endo-tracheal
4. CO2 -Carbon Dioxide

40. Evening shift

1. Leviticus 19:18; Romans 12:19
2. Captain and Tennille – pop artists in the mid-'70s

41. The Trip

1. Sammy Snead – an old-time golfer
2. Marv Alpert - a former announcer for the Knicks

42. Night Shift

1. ENT – Ear, Nose, and Throat
2. MIA – Missing In Action

43. Susie

1. Colossians 3:23
2. MVA – Motor Vehicle Accident
3. ET – Endo-tracheal
4. NG – Naso-gastric

44. The AHA

1. Psalm 135.6

45. Eduardo

1. Divorce - Malachi 2:13-16 and Matthew 19:3-9.

48. Moving On

1. Vol. I, Chapter 25
2. - Ephesians 2:8-9.
3. AHA – Alphabet Hikers of America – see Chapter 44 of Vol. 2
4. - Romans 5:8.

49. Val Again

1. - Matthew 5:33-34 or James 5:12.
2. - Ephesians 2:8-9.
3. Exodus 20:14.
4. Malachi 2:16 (NKJ)
5. Exodus. 20:16.

50. The Adventure

1. Nancy – his wife
2. Mel Brooks – a movie maker of many comedies
3. Ron Luciano – a flamboyant umpire, then

51. The Second Time

1. High Point – a NJ state park where NJ, NY, an PA meet
2. El Diablo – the devil.

52. The Divorce

1. Poconos – a popular resort in the Pennsylvania mountains
2. For an "A" – for the Alphabet Hikers of America – see Chapter 86 of this volume.
3. - Malachi 2:16 and Matthew 19:9.

Made in the USA
Columbia, SC
28 August 2023

22217489R00161